T0208967

Jesus
Is
There

Discovering
Jesus at Work
in the
Old Testament

Carl B. Dodrill, Ph.D.

WESTBOW
PRESS®
A DIVISION OF THOMAS NELSON
& ZONDERVAN

WestBow Press books may be ordered through booksellers or by contacting:

WestBow Press
A Division of Thomas Nelson & Zondervan
1663 Liberty Drive
Bloomington, IN 47403
www.westbowpress.com
844-714-3454

ISBN: 978-1-6642-3439-0 (sc)
ISBN: 978-1-6642-3440-6 (hc)
ISBN: 978-1-6642-3438-3 (e)

Library of Congress Control Number: 2021909572

Print information available on the last page.

WestBow Press rev. date: 06/08/2021

To my loving wife, Halie
whose unfailing support, Biblical knowledge, and practical advice
have been of immeasurable value in composing this manuscript

Contents

Preface

Is it possible that Jesus has been actively involved in interacting with and caring for people since they were created and placed in the Garden of Eden? Exploring this possibility is the topic of this book, but it has not been a topic that the vast majority of Christians have considered in any serious way. Even solid and well-read Christians assume that Jesus had personal contacts with people on a continuing basis on the earth only during his incarnation, about 33 years, of which his actual ministry was approximately three years. If Jesus hugely cares for people and to the point that he would give up his life for them, why has he been with them for only a few years among the thousands of years that they have walked on the earth? Is there any chance he has been with them more and we have just missed it?

My interest in the Old Testament goes back to my college days where at Westmont College I sat under Old Testament Professor David Hubbard. He was, in fact, my advisor my first year at the college. This interest in the Old Testament has continued through more than 40 years of teaching Sunday School and Bible classes, including teaching on Jesus in the Old Testament with my wife, Halie. Many favorable contacts with Jewish people have also been of assistance and will be referred to through the book. As a consequence of these and other factors, I have definitely felt led to consider a broader and deeper understanding of our Savior than I have ever had before. I trust you will join me as we together explore this possibility in what I hope will prove to be a vigorously interesting study.

The outstanding benefit of this study is to get us all to think more broadly and deeply about our Savior. Since you have picked up this book, more likely than not you are a Christian and you probably already have a solid understanding of Jesus. The chances are also good that your knowledge of Jesus is based first of all on the gospels which record his teachings and actions during the approximately three year period of his ministry. Yes, the gospels record all you need to know about Jesus, but since he is really divine, is there not a great deal more to learn about him that extends well beyond the gospels? True, the rest of the New Testament provides additional insights into Christ, but would you like to know more? And, would your view of Jesus be greatly enlarged if you could see him actively working with people for centuries before he was born in Bethlehem? A truly enriched and broadened understanding of your Savior is a major benefit that may come to you from this study.

Most Christians have not thought very much about what Jesus was doing during Old Testament times, and a few people seem to believe that Jesus did not even exist until he was born as a baby in Bethlehem. Fortunately, most Christians know that this is not true and that God is not ruled by time. We also know that Jesus was vitally involved in the creation of the universe (John 1:3; Colossians 1:16–17; Hebrews 1:2). Furthermore, Jesus bears the exact representation of God, he is one with God, all things exist through him and God jointly, and he lived before the foundation of the world was set (John 5:18, 10:30; 1 Corinthians 8:6; Ephesians 1:4; Colossians 1:15; Hebrews 1:3). Many other scriptures could be quoted, and a summary of the arguments on the eternality of Christ has been presented in detail.[1] However, nothing here tells us what Jesus was doing during the thousands of years before Bethlehem.

Some Christians will point to the likelihood that Jesus did appear in Old Testament times on a very occasional basis—*Christophanies*. I believe this to be true and I join these Christians in an emphasis on these appearances. However, these were intermittent occurrences with substantial periods of time between them. What was he doing between those appearances? Christians have also pointed to the *prophecies* of Christ in the Old Testament with regard to Jesus' coming and many have emphasized the *foreshadowings* of Christ's coming including *typologies* of Christ as seen in Old Testament characters. *Fulfillments* of the Old Testament in the life of Christ have also been emphasized as has a system of *covenant theology* which shows how Christ is revealed in the Old Testament

---

[1] Thomas C. Oden, *The Word of Life: Systematic Theology* (San Francisco: Harper Collins, 1992), 2:66–74.

covenants.[2] All of these areas of study are truly worthwhile, but in none of them is there a focused look at the possibility that Jesus might have been frequently involved with people on the earth during Old Testament times.

At this point it really must be mentioned that the fundamental idea of Christ being truly active with people in Old Testament times has occasionally appeared in the history of Christianity. For example, a very early church father was Justin Martyr (100-165) whose Logos Christianity clearly found Jesus as actively at work in the Old Testament.[3] The early Latin Church father, Tertullian (c160–c230) expressed this fundamental idea as well.[4] In his *Institutes of the Christian Religion*, John Calvin made clear his belief that God manifested himself repeatedly to the key figures of the Old Testament through the Son and Son only.[5] A more recent and emphatic statement of this position was made by John Walvoord (1969),[6] and in the 21st century a similar position has been taken by David Murray (2013) who discussed the topic in detail.[7] All these authors have been clear in their beliefs of Christ being very active with people in Old Testament times, but the expression of this idea has nevertheless been infrequent in Christian literature and it has never become popular.

One concern which has been expressed to me is whether a study of Jesus in the Old Testament would distract from studies of him during his incarnation. However, those studies have as a major objective an understanding of the nature and character of our Savior, and the Old Testament may help to meet that very objective by bringing in scriptures which can now be looked at in new ways. For example, if you become convinced that Jesus was centrally involved in more than a dozen passages in the Old Testament, wouldn't that provide you with a virtual goldmine

---

[2] Fulfillments are spelled out in Christopher J. H. Wright, *Knowing Jesus through the Old Testament* (Downers Grove, IL: Inter Varsity Press, 2014). Covenant theology is detailed in Daniel W. McManigal, *Encountering Christ in the Covenants: an Introduction to Covenant Theology* (West Linn, OR: Monergism Books, 2013).

[3] David E. Wilhite, "Is Jesus YHWH?: Two De-Judaizing Trajectories of Marcion and Justin," *Forum* 9, no. 1 (2000): 29-56.

[4] Cited by David Murray, *Jesus on Every Page* (Nashville: Thomas Nelson, 2013), 76–77.

[5] John Calvin, *Institutes* 4.8.5, John T. McNeill, ed., trans. by Ford Lewis Battles (Philadelphia: Westminster Press, 1960), 349.

[6] John F. Walvoord, *Jesus Christ Our Lord* (Chicago: Moody Publishers, 1969), 53.

[7] Murray, *Jesus on Every Page*, 73–85.

of scriptures to study so that you could understand him better? Surely, you would gain new insights! And what if a pastor, upon becoming equally convinced, offered a series of sermons on Jesus in the Old Testament? That would be a first for most of us as almost none of us have ever heard a single sermon on this topic despite decades of church attendance. It is fair to ask why this is the case, and this question will be answered in the first chapter of this book.

You may be wondering if this study is going to be based on humanly derived theories and postulations or on the Bible itself. Without a doubt, this study is based squarely on the word of God. True, it utilizes human understanding, logic, and some interesting techniques to approach the Bible. Yes, these are based on my experience and knowledge as your author, but all of them are directly anchored in the scriptures. All quotes from the Bible are from the *New International Version* (Zondervan, 2011). Bullet points at the end of every chapter except the last summarize the essential conclusions of that chapter. PAUSE sections are designed to get everyone to stop and consider the implications of what has just been presented, and they are especially good for group discussions.

As I have a long college and university academic background, much of the book has been written with all levels of students of the Bible in mind. The material is provocative and it can scarcely be read without questions being raised. Hopefully, these questions will lead to biblical searches and to the examination of other materials related to the topics under study. The desire is that each person who reads this book will wrestle with the ideas presented with the end result that thinking will be advanced and spiritual insights will be deepened.

I wish to thank my Editor, Susan Kipper, for solid assistance with the manuscript on many levels from the start to the very end. I also wish to thank the people who reviewed the entire manuscript and who provided a huge number of truly important suggestions. They include the Rev. Dr. Delmar Sewall, Nancy Roseen, Rev. Gary Risdon, Rev. David Jewett, and Rev. Shiv Muthukumar. Charles Van der Pool provided a scholarly review of the chapter on the Septuagint. Linda Gadola and Dale Dodrill gave useful grammatical and formatting information.

In conclusion, I hope that the study at hand will challenge you to think more broadly about your Savior and in particular about his involvement and concern for people going clear back to the Garden of Eden. You may find that this study will not just pay off from an increased knowledge viewpoint, but also that, with the leading of the Holy Spirit, you may arrive at a much deeper understanding of how much the Savior has always cared for people, and in particular how much he cares for you.

Carl B. Dodrill, Ph.D.
Mercer Island, Washington, USA
carl@dodrill.net
May, 2021

One

Why Do We Rarely See Jesus as Active in the Old Testament?

I know of no Christian who would not say that God the Father is active in the Old Testament. Further, "the Spirit of God," "the Spirit of the Lord," and similar terms are mentioned so many times that nearly anyone who has studied these occurrences would readily agree that the Holy Spirit is truly at work in the Old Testament. Why is it, then, that we seem to have such difficulty seeing Jesus as actively involved in the Old Testament and especially with

> **Factors Relevant to Seeing Jesus in the Old Testament**
>
> Doctrine of the Trinity
> Doctrine of the Incarnation
> Assumed equality of "God" and "Lord"
> Old and New Testaments seen as very different

people? Was he really not involved, or was he involved and for various reasons we have not seen that involvement? Let us explore the latter possibility by first reviewing two of the most relevant doctrines of the Christian faith and then by examining other factors that may have made it more difficult for us to see Jesus at work in the Old Testament.

Doctrine of the Trinity

The doctrine of the Trinity asserts that God exists in three persons: God the Father (first person of the Trinity), God the Son (second person of the Trinity, Jesus), and God the Holy Spirit (third person of the Trinity). There is only one God, but different aspects of him are discernable even in the first chapters of Genesis. God is complex; his ways go beyond understanding, and one cannot describe him well by postulating a simple single, indivisible personality. Recognizing these complexities and attempting to describe them does not mean that one is proposing the existence of more than one deity. Rather, it is an effort to grasp our glorious and multifaceted God whose nature extends beyond human understanding.

The doctrine of the Trinity can be viewed as an effort to recognize at least some of the depths of God's nature. The complexities of the Almighty can be viewed in three constellations which are personalities of the same God. This doctrine was formalized at the First Council of Nicaea in 325 CE. A total of 318 people attended this council, and an important result was the Nicene Creed, which is presented in table 1. It is worth studying this document because it gives the basics of who the three persons are that constitute the Trinity and what each of them does.

Our view of the almighty God is hugely influenced by the doctrine of the Trinity, and fundamental to the doctrine is that while each of the three members of the Trinity is God, they are distinguishable from each other. The importance of these core beliefs has been recognized for centuries, and in the middle ages, an interesting diagram portraying the Trinity was created. It is called the *Shield of the Trinity* and it points to the fundamental commonality of the three persons of the Trinity being God while at the same time clearly indicating that each person is different and distinguishable from the others.[8] This is directly relevant to our study since our detecting the work of Jesus in the Old Testament really hinges on our ability to distinguish between his work and that of the other persons of the Trinity.

A detailed discussion of the doctrine of the Trinity is not within the scope of this book nor is a detailed presentation of scriptural proofs of the doctrine. However, of particular interest are passages that refer to all

---

[8] The *Shield of the Trinity* is described in numerous places including Thomas Oden, *The Living God: Systematic Theology* (San Francisco: Harper/Collins, 1992), 220-21.

three members of the Trinity in the same verses (Matthew 3:16–17, Matthew 28:19–20, and 2 Corinthians 13:14).

> **2 Corinthians 13:14**
>
> May the grace of the Lord Jesus Christ, and the love of God, and the fellowship of the Holy Spirit be with you all.

Table 1. The Nicene Creed
First Council of Nicaea, 325 CE

We believe in one God
The Father, the Almighty, maker of heaven and earth, of all that is seen and unseen.
We believe in one Lord, Jesus Christ
The only Son of God, eternally begotten of the Father, God from God, Light from Light,
    true God from true God, begotten, not made, of one Being with the Father;
    through him all things were made.
    For us and for our salvation he came down from heaven, was incarnate of the Holy Spirit and the Virgin Mary
    and became truly human. For our sake he was crucified under Pontius Pilate;
    he suffered death and was buried. On the third day he rose again
    in accordance with the Scriptures; he ascended into heaven and is seated at the
    right hand of the Father. He will come again in glory to judge the living and the dead,
    and his kingdom will have no end.
We believe in the Holy Spirit, the Lord, the giver of life,
    who proceeds from the Father and the Son,
    who with the Father and the Son is worshiped and glorified,
    who has spoken through the prophets.
We believe in the one holy catholic and apostolic church.
We acknowledge one baptism for the forgiveness of sins.
We look for the resurrection of the dead, and the life of the world to come. Amen.

The above paragraphs present ample evidence for the doctrine of the Trinity, and for Christians no more proof is needed. But there is one major point here, and this is that Christians find evidence for the Trinity almost only in the New Testament. Obviously, God in three persons existed during Old Testament times, so why can we not find clearer evidence for the Trinity in the Old Testament? We can find God the Father and the Holy Spirit, so why not God the Son?

The best effort that I know of to find the Trinity in the Old Testament was made by Thomas Oden.[9] In six pages of intense analysis both of Old Testament passages and of the opinions of the early church fathers, Dr. Oden presents the best evidence he can find for the Trinity in the Old Testament. He then admits that "the triune teaching is never explicitly set forth in the Old Testament," and he also admits that it is odd that this is the case (p. 192). He then goes on to easily present 30 pages of proofs of the Trinity from the New Testament.

As early as the second century CE, Irenaeus hypothesized a form of progressive revelation in which the Old Testament merely prepared the way for the full revealing of the Trinitarian doctrine in the New Testament.[10] Possibly so, but perhaps we are putting a limitation on the Old Testament by simply not seeing the Trinity when it is there. In particular, we have difficulty in distinguishing between the person and work of God the Father and God the Son in the Old Testament. If we cannot make that distinction in the Old Testament, then there is no real way in which we can discern the work of the second person of the Trinity there. Therefore, a major focus of our study will be on sharpening our skills in making that distinction.

Doctrine of the Incarnation

Christians regularly believe that even though he was divine, the second person of the Trinity took on human flesh, was born as a baby like the rest of us, grew up, and became a man. As the supreme mediator between God and humanity, he then died, paying for our sins. This doctrine of the Incarnation is the cornerstone of our faith and of our salvation. In

---

[9] Oden, *The Living God*, 188–224.

[10] Irenaeus. *Against Heresies*, IV.32, ANF I, pp. 511ff. Cited in Oden, *The Living God, 192*.

embracing this doctrine, however, two limitations are often unintentionally placed on Jesus.

1. The Belief That Jesus Only Walked the Earth Once

Because Jesus walked the earth during a period of about 33 years, it is commonly assumed that this was the only time he ever came to earth. It is not as though we would say that he could not have walked on the earth before that time, but, well, he just did not do so—that is the kind of view that most Christians hold. This view not only holds now, but the view has been in place for hundreds of years. For example, the

> **Westminster Confession (1647)**
>
> The Son of God, the second person in the Trinity, being very and eternal God, of one substance and equal with the Father, did, when the fullness of time was come, take upon Him man's nature, with all the essential properties and common infirmities thereof, yet without sin: being conceived by the power of the Holy Ghost, in the womb of the virgin Mary, of her substance.

Westminster Confession of Faith (1647) is a hugely important confessional statement. In this document the first report of the appearance of Jesus on earth is at his birth by the Virgin Mary.[11] Thus, there is no recognition of an earlier appearance, and the belief is that he could not have come earlier since "the fullness of time" had not yet come. Are we sure that we should put this limitation on Jesus? Where does the Bible say that because the second person of the Trinity did appear incarnate at Bethlehem that therefore he could not have appeared at other times?

Note that the limitation just referred to does not even allow for the occasional bodily appearances by the second person of the Trinity called *Christophanies*. These appearances include events such as the Lord appearing to Abraham (Genesis 18), Jacob (Genesis 32), Balaam and his donkey (Numbers 22), Gideon (Judges 6), Samson's parents (Judges 13), and others.

---

[11] *Westminster Confession of Faith* (1647), Chapter VIII, Section II. From the manuscript of Cornelius Burges, Assessor to the Westminster Assembly, published in the modern edition of 1937 by S.W. Carruthers, accessed April, 2021, https://www.ligonier.org/learn/articles/westminster-confession-faith/. The complete *Confession* is also reproduced in many books and often with extensive notes. One of these is *The Confessions of Our Faith*, Brian W. Kenney, ed., (Indianapolis: Tanglewood Publishing, 2012).

While our study will support these appearances, it will go well beyond these by providing evidence that the second person of the Trinity frequently worked with people during Old Testament times. In order to consider this, you are invited to put aside the viewpoint of a single appearance of Christ in order to see what the Bible actually says about this matter.

2. The Assumption of Space and Time Limitations of Jesus' Body

We tend to think of Jesus in the same way as he appears in the gospels, in a physical body with the space and time limitations that our bodies have. True, during his incarnation he was able to do some things in his body that we cannot do, such as escaping from an angry crowd by going right through it (Luke 4), walking on water (John 6), and being transfigured (Luke 9). However, these miraculous events do not change our fundamental view of Jesus as a man with a body having the same space and time limitations as ours. That needs to be rethought, because when we consider any possibility of Jesus appearing in bodily form in the Old Testament, it is easy for us to put physical and time-related limitations on him when there is no scriptural support for such assumptions outside the period of his incarnation.

Even before his ascension into heaven, consider what Jesus did with his resurrection body, and it will be evident that his body was not limited by time or space. The story regarding the road to Emmaus is an excellent example of this (Luke 24). When Jesus blessed the bread at the table, his followers recognized who he was and he simply vanished out of their sight. Poof! He was gone. Shortly thereafter, he suddenly appeared to the eleven disciples in Jerusalem, going through the walls and/or the locked doors of the house they were in. And yes, Jesus had real flesh and blood as shown by his invitation to the disciples to see and touch him, and also by his eating food.

Even if one considers only the Emmaus incident, it is clear that Jesus was not constrained by a body with time and space limitations outside his incarnation period. If not so constrained, then during Old Testament times he was entirely able to suddenly appear at a particular spot on the earth, talk, touch people, eat food, and just as quickly vanish. If we can just get ourselves in the habit of seeing him in this way, the limitations in our thinking can be removed which we have unconsciously put on our Savior, limitations related to but not intended by the doctrine of the incarnation. Jesus can appear in bodily form any time and in any place he wishes, including appearing to people in Old Testament times.

Assumed Interchangeability of "God" and "Lord"

The words "God" and "Lord" are used in the Bible from Genesis to Revelation and they appear thousands of times. However, the vast majority of Christians do not distinguish between them, and they do not consider the possibility that these two words may not have the same meanings. Thus, the words are treated as interchangeable, but if they are truly interchangeable, why not just one word? Why would each word appear in the Bible thousands of times if it is essentially identical to another word? I believe that the particular words that are in the Bible are put in there for reasons and according to a divine plan. What is that plan for these two words, why are they there, and what have we been missing if we do not recognize the differences between them?

In this book, you will be invited to consider the possibility that recognizing the difference between "God" and "Lord" is a pivotal key to finding the presence of Christ in the Old Testament. In chapter 3, we will come to an understanding as to why we have these two words so many times in our Bibles and not a dozen Hebrew names for God. In chapter 4, we will study these two words intensively in the New Testament and insights will come to light as to whom these words actually refer. And then, in chapter 5, we will study these two words in the Old Testament, bringing to that study what we have learned in chapter 4. If you follow these studies closely and with the guidance of the Holy Spirit, you may find that in fact you have discovered a new way to find the second person of the Trinity in the Old Testament.

Old and New Testaments Seen as Very Different

A huge disconnect is felt by many Christians between the Old Testament and the New Testament with the result that the Bible is not seen as a unified work at all, but rather as a book consisting of two distinctly different documents. Many Christians tend to associate the Old Testament with God the Father, violence, killing, and injustice. Quite on the other hand, they associate the New Testament with Jesus, love, and the resolution of problems without resorting to violence. There is also a tendency to see the New Testament as concerned with various social inequities and with peace. Given these remarkably different views of the Old Testament and the New Testament, there is resistance to seeing Jesus as being significantly connected with the Old Testament. How could a person who has come to earth to bring peace and love be associated in any significant way with the Old Testament with all the killing, violence, and misery that are to be found there?

One outstanding intention of this book is to point to the unity of the Bible. It is not believed that God promoted two books with significantly different objectives and standards. Oddly enough, it is Jesus himself who offers information in the New Testament which provides key links between the Old and New Testaments. Indeed, on numerous occasions he quoted Old Testament passages in his teachings, explicating them, reinforcing them, and never taking exception to them. Some of those passages are difficult and uncomfortable, but he does not soften them. The thing that is remarkable here is that Jesus does the very same thing in the New Testament in his own teachings by not softening them, not making them more socially acceptable, and not presenting a picture dominated by love and peace. Here are some of Jesus' teachings in the New Testament which illustrate the basic points at hand:

> **Matthew 10:34–36**
>
> Do not suppose that I have come to bring peace to the earth. I did not come to bring peace, but a sword. For I have come to turn "a man against his father, a daughter against her mother, a daughter-in-law against her mother-in-law—a man's enemies will be the members of his own household."

1. Jesus Did Not Come to Bring Peace

Jesus did not come to bring peace but a sword and divisions among people, even to the point of families being divided (Matthew 10:34–36; Luke 12:51–53). When some people are believers and some are not, this disharmony is clearly shown, and while he would wish for peace among the peoples of the world, there is no evidence that his mission to earth was to bring it. Peace with God, yes, by dying on the cross, and, peace among believers (Mark

9:50; Luke 2:14, 24:36; John 14:27, 20:19, 21 & 26). But not necessarily peace generally among the nations, among racial groups, and across other dimensions which result in divisions among people such as gender and socioeconomic status.

2. Inequitable Landowner

Jesus portrayed the kingdom of heaven like a landowner who hired workers for greatly different periods of time (1 to 12 hours) but paid them all the same (Matthew 20:1–16). This is not fair by today's cultural standards—it should be "equal pay for equal work." But in verse 15, Jesus says, "Don't I have the right to do what I want with my own money?" Jesus even ends the section with, "So the last will be first, and the first will be last." These standards do not set well with twenty-first century western minds, but they are the teachings of Jesus, and when we find similar differences in standards in the Old Testament, we need to take the time to understand them rather than being put off by them.

3. Unequal Access to the Truth

Jesus often spoke so that only people with spiritual eyes and ears given to them by God would understand what he was saying (Matthew 13:10–16; Mark 4:10–12; Luke 8:9–10). From these passages, it is clear that not everyone has equal access to spiritual truths, and at times Jesus even seems happy to know that some things have

> **Matthew 13:11 & 13**
>
> The knowledge of the secrets of the kingdom of heaven has been given to you, but not to them… This is why I speak to them in parables: "Though seeing, they do not see; though hearing, they do not hear or understand."

been hidden. Consider, for example, the account recorded at the time he sent out 72 of his followers: "At that time Jesus, full of joy through the Holy Spirit, said, 'I praise you, Father, Lord of heaven and earth, because you have hidden these things from the wise and learned, and revealed them to little children.'" (Luke 10:21)

4. Narrow and Wide Gates

Consider the teaching on the narrow and wide gates (Matthew 7:13–14). The gate and road that leads to life are narrow, and few find it. But, the path to destruction is easy to find and many do. Wait a minute— should it not be easy to find salvation and should not everyone have an equal chance at finding it? So, the New Testament does not conform to the standards of our culture and our era of time, but Jesus is central to the New Testament. So, why can he not also be active in the Old Testament even when the teachings there also do not conform?

> **Matthew 7:13–14**
>
> Enter through the narrow gate. For wide is the gate and broad is the road that leads to destruction, and many enter through it. But small is the gate and narrow the road that leads to life, and only a few find it.

5. Parable of the Tenants

The parable of the tenants is found in Mark 12:1–12. A landlord prepares a property, leases it out to tenants and goes away. When he sends servants for some of the fruit of the vineyard, the tenants beat up the servants, and when he sends his own son believing they will respect him, they kill the son. So, the landlord comes back and kills the tenants without giving them a chance to explain their actions. It is easy for us to raise questions about whether or not this is just, but this story is a picture of God doing what is right and we need to give him permission to do what he wishes rather than criticizing him like judges.

6. Jesus as Judge

I do not know anyone who likes to think of Jesus as a judge, but in John 5:22 & 27, it is clear that God the Father has given the second person of the Trinity the power to judge: "Moreover, the Father judges no one, but has entrusted all judgment to the Son" (John 5:27). Further, in the final judgment, it is Jesus who will sit on the throne and pronounce judgment on both the righteous and the unrighteous (Matthew 25:31–46). The unrighteous will be condemned to the eternal fire prepared for the devil and his angels. I do not find anything this severe in the entire

Old Testament and certainly not worse than this teaching. What all this means is that when we get to the Old Testament and find the divine in a judgmental role, we cannot therefore automatically dismiss such passages as being unrelated to the second person of the Trinity. On the contrary, being a judge is clearly one of roles of Jesus, and his love for people does not nullify this judgmental role.

All of these teachings of our Lord in the New Testament are difficult for us to deal with, and there is a tendency for our churches and our pastors to skip over them or minimize them. But, they are the teachings of Jesus, and when we find similar teachings in the Old Testament, we cannot be put off by them. Indeed, if we study the difficult teachings in both the Old and New Testaments, we will be impressed with their similarities rather than their differences.

Conclusions

In this introductory chapter, we have addressed the question as to why it is that we rarely (or never) see Jesus as active in the Old Testament. We have found the following:

- In the New Testament we can quite easily distinguish the work of the three members of the Trinity. In the Old Testament, however, we have trouble especially discerning the work of the second person of the Trinity. That has led to the opinion that he was not active in Old Testament times, but perhaps we do not know how to identify his work and have therefore often missed it.
- The Doctrine of the Incarnation has unfortunately led to the assumption that because Jesus came to earth once on a divinely timed basis that he could not have been on earth at any other time. It is also easy to assume that the physical limitations Jesus had during the incarnation must exist at other times as well. These assumptions lack biblical foundations, and by putting them aside, we will be better able to see Jesus on earth whenever and wherever he wishes to appear.
- The words "God" and "Lord" in the Bible are commonly assumed to be interchangeable, but our studies will show that they are

differences between them in the persons to whom they refer. Understanding these differences will prove to be a major key in distinguishing between the first and second persons of the Trinity in the Old Testament.

- Insights about the unity of the Old and New Testaments into a single Bible are gained by studying the teachings of Jesus in the New Testament.

This chapter is intended to help us understand and put aside those things that have often kept Christians from finding Jesus at work in the Old Testament. We will now examine the history and development of rabbinical Judaism as it will pave the way to better grasping why Jesus said what he said and did what he did in the gospels.

Two

The Development of Rabbinical Judaism

Christians know that Jesus was Jewish, but they rarely think of him in that way and they almost never study Judaism in an effort to better understand their Savior. Nevertheless, this is exactly what I have done. Although I have taught Bible for more than 40 years, it is only in recent times that I realized that the Jews of today have remarkably similar beliefs and practices as the Jews had in the time of Jesus. True, there is no longer a temple and thus certain practices have ceased such as sacrifices. There are also a number of technological advances (such as the invention of electricity) which have required the Jews to make adjustments. Nevertheless, the beliefs and practices of Jews have continued with remarkable consistency over the centuries. Realizing this, and in an effort to understand Jesus better, on more than 30 occasions in the last three years I have attended Jewish classes and services at synagogues, I purchased my own kipah, and I have two men on a first name basis whom I call my rabbis! I have been welcomed into these Jewish settings without fail and I have never been made to feel ill at ease. Further, my wife and I routinely walk with a devout Jewish couple, and I have asked them hundreds of questions. This entire experience with Jewish people has been very positive and of great value to me. The first-hand understanding of Judaism which I have gained by this effort is combined with what we know about Jewish history in what follows.

A summary of Jewish history, included in this chapter as table 2, provides a quick overview on the history of God's chosen people. Dating is somewhat problematic prior to 1000 BCE, but approximate dates can be obtained for earlier events if one literally interprets 1 Kings 6:1. That verse says that there were 480 years from the exodus from Egypt to the fourth year of King Solomon's reign. Using this information and then figuring backwards, Abraham must have been alive in the year 2000 BCE, Moses in 1500 BCE, King David in 1000 BCE, and Ezra in 500 BCE. The exodus from Egypt was then approximately 1446 BCE, and the giving of the law at Sinai approximately 1441 BCE. As 1 Kings 6:1 is often not taken literally, all of these dates are somewhat earlier than those commonly cited by scholars today. However, the differences are not of significance for our study.

Table 2. Overview of Jewish history			
Date	Emphasis	Outstanding Person	Major Events
2000 BCE	People	Abraham	• Era of the patriarchs (Abraham, Isaac, Jacob) • Spiritual decline • Bondage in Egypt
1500 BCE	Land	Moses	• Exodus from Egypt (c1446) • The Law given (c1441) • Conquest of promised land begins (c1405) • Period of the judges; spiritual decline
1000 BCE	Kingdom	David	• United kingdom: Saul, David, Solomon (1050–930) • Civil war divides kingdom—Israel and Judah (930) • Assyria conquers Israel (732) • Babylon conquers Judah (586) • Cyrus conquers Babylon (539) • First exiles return to Judah from Babylon (538)
500 BCE	Remnant	Ezra	• Esther becomes queen in Persia (c459) • Second group of exiles returns under Ezra (458) • Malachi prophesies (440–430)

				• Nehemiah brings back the last group of exiles (432) • Israel ruled by Persia until c330, ruled by Greece from c330–167, and ruled by Rome from 37 through the 2nd century CE • Pharisees, Sadducees, Zealots, Essenes appear • Translation of Septuagint (LXX) begins (c280) • Apocrypha and pseudepigrapha started (c250) • Temple profaned (Dec. 167) and Maccabean revolt • Hasmonean dynasty, Jews independent (c142–37) • Jesus born in Bethlehem (c6–2 BCE)
CE begins				• Jewish rebellion against Rome (66–73) • Jerusalem and the temple destroyed (70) • Final Jewish rebellion crushed by Rome (132–136) • *Mishnah* compiled (c200) • Babylonian *Talmud* completed (c500)

NOTE: The dates in this table prior to 1000 BCE rest on a literal interpretation of 1 Kings 6:1 which says that there were 480 years from the exodus out of Egypt to the fourth year of King Solomon's reign.

In approximately 1050 BCE, the primary emphasis turned from settling God's people in the Promised Land to the establishment of the united kingdom. Unfortunately, civil war divided the kingdom by 930 BCE. Of huge significance was the conquering of the northern kingdom of Israel by Assyria in 732 BCE, and the conquering of the southern kingdom of Judah by Babylon in 586 BCE. Fortunately, Cyrus of Persia overthrew Babylon in 539 BCE and, directed by God, he allowed the return of Jewish exiles from Babylon to Jerusalem (Ezra 1). The first group returned the next year (538 BCE) and the second group under Ezra in 458 BCE.

The Special Significance of Ezra

A reading of the book of Ezra will launch us into an understanding of this part of Jewish history. This book shows that there was an overwhelming focus on the Law of the Lord when a number of the Jews came back from their captivity in Babylon in 458 BCE under the leadership of Ezra. Ezra had devoted himself to the

> **Letter from King Artaxerxes**
> **Ezra 7:25-26**
>
> And you, Ezra, in accordance with the wisdom of your God, which you possess, appoint magistrates and judges to administer justice to all the people of Trans-Euphrates—all who know the laws of your God. And you are to teach any who do not know them. Whoever does not obey the law of your God and the law of the king must surely be punished by death, banishment, confiscation of property, or imprisonment.

study, observance, and teaching of the law to the people of Israel (Ezra 7:10). In the letter which King Artaxerxes wrote to Ezra, he ordered Ezra to teach the Jewish laws and that anyone who did not obey the laws should be severely punished. This "blank check" handed to Ezra was applauded by Ezra in verses 27 and 28, and his mission was clearly in place.

A major question that Ezra and other Jewish leaders asked early on was why God would allow both the northern and southern kingdoms to be conquered by foreigners. They concluded that the reason was because the Jewish people had not followed the laws given to them by God. To remedy this, it was necessary first to determine what the laws were. Ezra and the Jewish leaders who followed first went through the Torah and identified each and every law they could find. They found 613. Since God obviously wanted his laws obeyed, obedience to them became the focus of the Jewish religious system, and if each law was appropriately interpreted and obeyed by the Jewish people, the capture of Jews by foreign powers should cease. As a consequence, Ezra and the rabbis who followed him examined every law, attempted to determine when the law was applicable, and exactly how the law was to be obeyed. The job took a very long time since each law deserved detailed consideration, and also as it was believed that many laws required multiple regulations be set up in order to promote proper observance of the law.

In the years between Ezra and the birth of Christ, important Jewish leader groups appeared, especially the Pharisees and the Sadducees. There is no question but that the primary focus of these groups was on the law and obedience to it. Building on the work of Ezra and others, the leaders in these groups continued to develop and refine rules and guidelines to make it difficult for the laws to be broken. While these rules and guidelines were not written down for hundreds of years, they increasingly became the essence of Judaism, both at the time of Christ and now. Furthermore, the teachers presenting these rules began to be called *rabbis*, and thus they developed *rabbinical Judaism*. They were not called priests in most cases because much of the time there was no temple available in which to perform priestly functions such as sacrifices.

Most of us in the Christian tradition do not have a real grasp of the impact upon Judaism of the hugely increased emphasis upon the law in the approximately 500 years before the birth of Christ. This emphasis resulted in the establishment of numerous rules and regulations by the rabbis, and it was these rules and regulations which became the guiding light for the everyday practice of Judaism. As a result, Judaism became what is best described as *rabbinical* and this is what it is today. While these rules and regulations were not written down at the time when Jesus was born, they were nevertheless well known. They were put in writing in about CE 200 as the *Mishnah*. The classical volume of the *Mishnah* detailing the rules and regulations presents approximately 8,300 rules and regulations in 800 pages.[12]

The vast majority of the rules and regulations presented in the *Mishnah* were definitely in place at the time of the ministry of Jesus, and the Jews lived by those traditions just as they do today. Furthermore, the Jewish leaders felt an obligation to monitor the behavior of the population because if people in general did not follow God's laws (interpreted as the rules and traditions that the elders had set up), that behavior could once again become the basis for the entire nation being hauled off into captivity. Jesus followed God's laws but not the rabbinical rules when they departed from God's laws. Frequent conflicts with the Jewish leaders resulted, and excellent summaries of these conflicts are presented in Matthew 15:1–9 and Mark 7:1–13. In those summaries, Jesus emphatically points to the

---

[12] Herbert Danby, *The Mishnah* (Oxford: Oxford University Press, 1933).

errors of the Jewish leaders especially including the abandonment of God's laws in favor of their own rules and traditions.

Matthew 15:1–9

Then some Pharisees and teachers of the law came to Jesus from Jerusalem and asked, "Why do your disciples break the tradition of the elders? They don't wash their hands before they eat!" Jesus replied, "And why do you break the command of God for the sake of your tradition? For God said, 'Honor your father and mother' and 'Anyone who curses their father or mother is to be put to death.' But you say that if anyone declares that what might have been used to help their father or mother is 'devoted to God,' they are not to 'honor their father or mother' with it. Thus you nullify the word of God for the sake of your tradition. You hypocrites! Isaiah was right when he prophesied about you: 'These people honor me with their lips, but their hearts are far from me. They worship me in vain; their teachings are merely human rules.'"

The Apostle Paul also unquestionably distanced himself from the "traditions of the elders." Galatians was among the earliest of Paul's epistles, and in the very first chapter he made this distancing very clear (Galatians 1:11–17). He indicated that before he became a Christian, he enthusiastically embraced the traditions of the Jewish elders, but when he received the revelation of Jesus Christ, those traditions were forever thrown off.

In my attendance at many Jewish classes and teaching sessions, I have found that the content consists primarily of studies of rabbinical opinions on whatever topic is under discussion. Sometimes there actually is no reading from the Torah at all, and when there is a reading, it is brief and introductory to a detailed consideration of rabbinical opinion on the topic at hand. Thus, the study is typically not on the Torah reading but on the intricacies of the interpretation of Torah section by one or more rabbis. Overall, the preeminence of rabbinical opinion is evident in Jewish thinking, and it is clear to me that were I to follow Judaism, I would need to have a solid contact with at least one rabbi whose opinions I could get so that I would know how to respond to various situations.

The Belief in the Oral Torah

Another concept in rabbinical Judaism which is firmly in place is the *Oral Torah*. The belief here is that when God gave the law to Moses on Mt. Sinai, he also gave a series of instructions on when the particular laws were to be obeyed, how they were to be obeyed, and even why the laws were given to begin with. The full development of this belief includes the idea that Moses was told <u>not</u> to write all of these things down, and instead that he was directed to pass down this information orally through the lines of Jewish leaders. First, it went to Joshua, then on to Pinchas, Eli, Shemuel, David, Achiah, Elijah, to Elisha and so on down through the generations of leaders. These are the first several of 40 generations of leaders who were said to have gotten the *Oral Torah*, the last of which was Rabbi Ashi who lived in 352 to 427 CE.[13] By then it had been written down in the *Mishnah*, and no more oral transmission was necessary.

Common Jewish terms
Rabbi—Jewish teacher; authorized to make decisions on issues of Jewish law
Oral Torah—unwritten instructions given by God to Moses and handed down orally along with rabbinical teachings until put in writing as the *Mishnah*
Mishnah—written form of the *Oral Torah*; appeared about CE 200
Gemara—commentary on the *Mishnah*
Talmud—the most significant collection of the Jewish oral tradition including the Mishnah and the *Gemara*; interprets the Torah
Torah—first five books of the Old Testament

Most Christians have never even heard of the existence of the *Oral Torah* nor do they understand what it espouses. Once I understood it, I had great difficulty with it both because its origin is immediately in question and also because its authority and content are not consistent with Christianity. In fact, there is no evidence for the existence of the *Oral Torah* in the entire Old Testament as there is not even a single reference to it. I have heard some Jews frankly admit that this is true. Nevertheless, they ascribe a very high level of importance to the *Oral Torah*. In a six week class I took on basic Judaism, it was the very first topic discussed, it was

---

[13] Jewish Learning Institute, *Judaism Decoded: The Origins and Evolution of Jewish Tradition* (Brooklyn: The Rohr Jewish Learning Institute, 2015), 32–33.

by far the biggest topic covered throughout the class, and it was clear that rabbinical Judaism and the authority of the rabbis hinge heavily on it.[14]

Jews point out that there are many laws given without details about how to carry them out, and that the Hebrew Scriptures do not give enough information to do so. As one basic Jewish textbook says, the written Torah is "insufficient."[15] For example, if the written Torah says that a certain animal should be sacrificed, exactly how should it be done is not specified nor is what time of day or year should it be done, who should do it, who should provide the animal, what if the providers cannot pay, what if they live too far from Jerusalem where the sacrifice should be done, or what should be done if the nation is at war at the moment. Further, the Hebrew Scriptures rarely say why a particular law has been put in place, and it is believed that such explanations are needed. Finally, a considerable amount of time is spent by the Jews defending the reliability of oral transmission with the conclusion that it is not only reliable but in some ways it is superior to the written text. This is puzzling to most people but they claim that every time the oral tradition was passed down, it was explained and questions could be asked in great detail and to the point that the new receiver of the information had a thorough understanding of it. Thus, it is postulated that there is a fuller understanding of the *Oral Torah* than the written Torah which in contrast had no one to explain it and which has therefore has been subject to various interpretations over the centuries.

If you accept the concept of the *Oral Torah,* you provide a valid place for the teachings of the rabbis. Further, those teachings are given authority right alongside the Old Testament or even superior to it. The significance of this last point should not be overlooked. When the *Oral Torah* was put in writing as the *Mishnah* in about CE 200, a basis was provided for the rabbis to offer commentary. Rabbis did so heavily from CE 200 to CE 500, and the commentary of those in Babylonia has been considered especially authoritative. That commentary is called the *Gemara*, and when that commentary is combined with the *Mishnah*, the *Talmud* resulted and the most popular form of it from Babylon appeared in about CE 500.

The most popular edition of the *Talmud* occupies 73 volumes, each of

---

[14] Jewish Learning Institute, *Judaism Decoded.*
[15] Jewish Learning Institute, *Judaism Decoded,* 5.

which is the size of a volume of an encyclopedia.[16] Each volume covers only a few pages of the *Mishnah* and offers extensive and highly detailed commentary on that section of the *Mishnah*. The *Talmud* is considered to be the apex of the Jewish faith and it is viewed as more authoritative than the Hebrew Scriptures alone. The *Talmud* has a basis in the written Torah, but it takes advantage of both the oral tradition and the commentaries of the most esteemed Jewish rabbis. Therefore it is considered to be superior to the written text. Serious Jews study the *Talmud* regularly and I myself have sat through about a dozen such one hour study sessions. The rabbi under whom I sat for these sessions has been teaching the *Talmud* for more than 30 years. Over the year and a half that I attended these studies, less than one volume was studied, a volume which covered only about 8 pages of the 800 page *Mishnah*. In those sessions, minutiae of Jewish law were examined in great detail with numerous quotes from various rabbis over the centuries but only rarely with a quote from the Torah. The belief is that there is no need to appeal to the Bible for authority as the *Talmud* has authority in and of itself.[17]

> **Jeffrey Radon, Jewish scholar**
>
> In terms of authority and from a legal point of view, we as Jews in traditional rabbinic Judaism live not by what is written in the Bible, but by the Bible as interpreted by the Jewish tradition, the foundation of which is the Talmud - and, in this sense the Talmud is more authoritative than the Bible.[15]

I found myself stunned time and time again with teachings such as those on the *Oral Torah* and the *Talmud* because they were so far afield from what we believe as Christians. Further, a check with Jews in the different groups (Orthodox, Conservative, Reformed) revealed that all hold to a fundamental belief in the validity and superiority of the *Oral Torah* and *Talmud*. It is no wonder that Jesus and the Apostle Paul said what they said in the New Testament to the Jewish leaders, and we now have a better understanding of why Jesus came down so hard on the Jewish leaders. It is worth your reading Matthew 23 at this point as it will give

---

[16] Jerome Schottenstein, *Talmud Bavli* (Brooklyn: Art Scroll Mesorah Publications, 1995), 73 vols.

[17] Jeffrey Radon, "Which is More Sacred for Jews, the Talmud or Tanakh?" Quora website, November 22, 2017. https://www.quora.com/Which-is-more-sacred-for-the-Jews-the-Talmud-or-Tanakh.

you a good idea of how far afield Jesus pronounced the Jewish traditions to be, and his comments are arguably his most severe in all the gospels.

Final Comments on the Law

As we come to the end of this chapter, one cannot help but make special note once again of the incredible emphasis that is placed on the law in Jewish teachings and traditions. Of the approximately 30 sessions of Jewish classes which I attended, at least 28 were on the law. Further, the entire *Talmud* is on the law, not on the rest of the Old Testament. It is clear that the emphasis in Judaism is on knowing and following God's commandments as interpreted by the rabbis. The rabbinical commentaries on the first five books of the Old Testament routinely get the attention in these studies, and the other books in the Old Testament far less. *Bar mitzvah* means "son of the commandment" and *bat mitzvah* means "daughter of the commandment" so that the passing of boys and girls into adulthood is framed out specifically as these young people taking on the law for their lives. Likewise, the Jewish prayer shawl has 613 tassels so that one symbolically surrounds oneself with the law when it is worn. This overwhelming emphasis on the law with only rare references to the love of God no doubt made it difficult for the Jews of Jesus' day to see Jesus for who he was. Unfortunately, this is still true.

Lastly, it is noted that the Jews lived successively under the rule of the Persians, the Greeks (three different Greek ruling systems), and the Romans. These rulings by foreigners were continuous from the time of Ezra up through the second century CE and beyond, the only exception being the Hasmonean dynasty from 142–37 BCE. Thus, the postulation of Ezra and other Jewish leaders that following the law would prevent foreign rule of Israel was sadly in error. Indeed, from the time of Christ onward, the Jews were not an independent self-ruling nation until 1948.

Conclusions

This chapter was intended to help us better understand Jewish beliefs and practices at the time of Christ in order to allow us to more fully grasp why he said what he said and did what he did in the gospels.

- A huge focus on the law is deeply rooted in Jewish belief and practice. This was true at the time of Christ and it is true today as well.
- Especially from the time of Ezra onward, the Jewish rabbis developed several thousand rules and regulations based on the 613 laws they found in the written Torah. Ultimately, these rabbinical laws were called the *Oral Torah*, and they were not written down at the time of Christ but only later as the *Mishnah*.
- The rabbinical rules and regulations became the "traditions of the elders" by which the Jews lived, and, as is true today, these rabbinical rules were considered to be superior to the written Torah.
- Jesus vehemently denounced these rabbinical traditions and the Jewish leaders who held them, and especially so when those traditions obscured or departed from the underlying intent of God's laws.

We now turn to a topic which is the least well-known in this book but which has some of the farthest reaching implications for finding Jesus in the Old Testament.

Three

The Incredibly Important Septuagint (LXX)

Thus far, we have looked at reasons why Christians often do not see Jesus in the Old Testament, and we have covered important background information on Jewish history. All of this has been done to lay down a foundation to help us find Jesus at work with people through the Old Testament. We now continue to lay down important facts to achieve this goal by examining the most important translation of the Old Testament from the Hebrew into Greek. It may surprise you that this translation will supply major help as we search for the work of the second person of the Trinity in Old Testament times.

In table 2 in the last chapter (page 14), it was noted that Israel was ruled by Greece from approximately 330 to 167 BCE, but the significance of this was not commented on. We now need to understand this period better in order to proceed. Alexander the Great was born in 356 BCE and he succeeded his father to the throne in Greece at the age of 20. Greek culture, language, philosophy, and military power were at their peak, and the Greeks were convinced that the world would be a better place if it adopted their culture and language. By that time, the huge impacts of Pythagoras, Socrates, Euclid, Plato, and Aristotle had been felt.

Soon after taking power, Alexander began a military campaign to spread Greek culture and language as far as possible into the civilized world. In just 13 years he took over huge areas of Europe, a significant portion of Asia extending as far east as India, and also the northern part of Africa. This meant conquering Persia which had controlled Israel back to the time of Ezra, and this brought Greek rule to Israel in about 330 BCE. The spread of Greek thinking and culture by Alexander resulted in an unprecedented era of Greek influence of at least 600 years (300 BCE–300 CE).

After Alexander died of a mysterious illness in 323 BCE, his generals divided up the kingdom. The first general to gain control of Palestine was Ptolemy (I) Soter who resided in Egypt and whose Greek government ruled Israel from 320 BCE to 198 BCE. This was a good period of time for the Jews because they were not oppressed by the Greeks, and it was far more favorable than under the Greek Seleucid group which followed. That group pushed Greek culture and language to the extreme, and their most notable ruler, Antiochus (IV) Epiphanes gained control of Israel in 175 BCE. He clamped down on the Jews and prohibited many aspects of Judaism including circumcision, observing the Sabbath, and the following of dietary laws. In 167 BCE, he slaughtered thousands of Jews, profaned the temple, and proclaimed Zeus as the official god. However, a successful rebellion against the Seleucids was led by Judas Maccabeus and in 164 BCE, Jerusalem was regained and the temple was cleansed and restored. This began the only period of Jewish independence for hundreds of years. In 37 BCE, the Romans took over and Jewish independence was brought to an end.

The Greeks had established in Egypt what was likely the most important library in the history of the world, and the Greek rulers there supported this library. Ptolemy Philadelphus (285–246 BCE) was ruler during a portion of the time that the Ptolemies ruled over Palestine, and he noticed that the Old Testament Hebrew scriptures were nowhere to be found in Greek. He sought to fill this gap in the library's collection by commissioning an official translation, but in order to meet scholarly standards, he had to ask the Jews to make the translation as they were the only people who knew Hebrew well. Stories (and legends) differ as to how and where he got the Jewish scholars to do the translation, but one frequently cited source (*Letter of Aristeas*) is that from Jerusalem he got six translators from each of the 12 tribes to do the translation, 72 in all. Other accounts say 70 translators but the accounts typically indicate that the translators were skilled Jewish scholars and rabbis. Indeed, it is not clear that there was anyone else with enough knowledge of written Hebrew to have done the translation. The ancient Greek title of the resulting document was "The Translation of the Seventy" and in English it is commonly called the *Septuagint* or LXX. In Roman numerals, LXX is an approximate figure both for the number of translators and for the 72 days said to be required to do the work.[18]

It is believed that the LXX translation of the Torah was either in progress or done by approximately 280 BCE, with the translation of the rest of the Old Testament without a clear date but possibly as early as the next 30–40 years.[19] The books of the Apocrypha were later added to the LXX, but these non-canonical texts need not concern us. It is noted that the topic at hand has a huge number of complexities to it including evidence for multiple translations with different translators, places of translation, and likely dates of translation. Fortunately, only a small portion of these complexities are relevant to our study, and the remainder will be put aside, but they are available to the interested student.[20] The objectives of this chapter are to provide a text readable by everyone including those with no knowledge whatsoever of Koine Greek, and at the same time to present to the most advanced LXX scholar ideas about the usefulness and validity of the LXX which have not been published previously.

The Remarkable Impacts of the Septuagint

The LXX was hugely influential with multiple impacts which lasted for centuries. We need to have a good understanding of these impacts because the LXX points us to the first of three keys that we will use to explore the possibility of Jesus being active with people on multiple occasions in Old

---

[18] The *Letter of Aristeas* is the one document repeatedly cited because it gives many details about the translation and the excellent situation and careful way in which it was done. The letter includes a list of the names of all 72 translators. While this letter has been criticized by scholars, it has not clearly been shown to be counter to historical facts regarding the translation and how it was conducted. The letter has been translated into English by R. Charles, and in April, 2021, accessed at https://www.ellopos.com/blog/4508/letter-of-aristeas-full-text-in-greek-and-english/26/.

[19] Merrill F. Unger, *Bible Dictionary* (Chicago: Moody Press, 1977), 1148. See also Introduction to *Septuagint Version of the Old Testament* (Grand Rapids: Zondervan, 1977), ii.

[20] Karen H. Jobes and Moisés Silva, *Invitation to the Septuagint* (Grand Rapids: Baker Academic, 2015).

Testament times. This key is not obvious on a brief reading of the history of the LXX, and it is therefore not surprising that its value has not been commonly recognized. The key was evident to me after I undertook extensive study of the LXX. For those with an interest in doing a similar study, I note that four sources were especially useful: 1) a truly in-depth and academic commentary on the LXX together with summaries of scholarly findings on a large number of factors and issues;[21] 2) an overall perspective on the LXX including its impacts on the New Testament;[22] 3) a major document comparing the LXX and the Hebrew Old Testament with the New Testament quotes of the Old Testament;[23] and, 4) a compilation of the views of early Christian theologians on the validity and inspiration of the LXX.[24]

> **Outstanding Features & Contributions of the LXX**
>
> 1. Early date and early recognition as authoritative
> 2. Led to the names "Jesus" and "Christ"
> 3. Reorganized the Hebrew Bible
> 4. Broadly influential for centuries
> 5. Provided the names we use today for God in both the Old and the New Testament
> 6. Criticisms of the LXX

Based on the sources just cited, five outstanding features and contributions of the LXX are now brought to your attention, and these will be followed by a review of the criticisms of the LXX.

1. Early Date and Early Recognition as Authoritative

There are four important considerations here.

---

[21] Jobes and Silva, *Invitation to the Septuagint.*

[22] Ragnar Osborn, "Considering the Septuagint: Today's Forgotten Book that Changed Human History" 2012, https://considerthegospel.org/2012/03/19/considering-the-septuagint-todays-forgotten-book-that-changed-human-history-part-1/. Part 2 and Session 6 are especially helpful.

[23] Jobes and Silva, *Invitation to the Septuagint*, 181-199. Also, see R. Grant Jones, "Notes on the Septuagint." July, 2000, online February, 2006, https://www.scribd.com/document/125854377/Jones-LXX-Notes-Feb06.

[24] Gabe Martini, "Is the Septuagint a Divinely Inspired Translation?" September, 2015, http://modeoflife.org/is-the-septuagint-a-divinely-inspired-translation/.

A. Early Date

With a portion or much of the LXX translated in the third century BCE, this is the earliest essentially complete translation of the Old Testament that exists. The earlier Hebrew text on which it was based has not been located except for a few limited documents from the same era that were found the in the Dead Sea Scrolls. Complete copies of the LXX are available today which date back to the fourth century CE, but by contrast, the complete Masoretic Hebrew manuscripts on which our Old Testament English translations are based go back to only the ninth century CE.[25] There is therefore a huge difference in the dating of these manuscripts. Thankfully, many Hebrew texts available today are faithful copies of earlier Old Testament manuscripts in Hebrew as has been shown by the Dead Sea Scrolls. However, it also appears that the LXX may agree better with some of the earliest (approximately third century BCE) fragmentary Hebrew Dead Sea Scrolls than do the later Hebrew texts.[26] If so, some changes in the Hebrew text over time may have occurred, there may have been more than one Hebrew manuscript at the time the LXX was translated, or both. The complexities here have been considered in great detail, and it is clear that conclusions in this area need to be drawn with great care.[27]

> **1. LXX—Early and Authoritative**
> A. Early date
> B. Highly qualified translators
> C. Early recognition
> D. Correction and clarification of the Hebrew text

In summary for this section on dating, the LXX unquestionably predates by hundreds of years the Masoretic Hebrew texts on which our Old Testament English translations are based. At least in some cases, the LXX may agree better with the earliest third century BCE fragmentary Hebrew documents that exist than do the later Hebrew manuscripts. A detailed scholarly examination of this topic is far beyond the scope of the present volume, but the Jewish scholars with whom I have had contact all agree that they do not know what happened to the Hebrew text during the centuries of political change and turmoil. As a consequence of all these

---

[25] Jobes and Silva, *Invitation to the Septuagint*, 157. Also, Osborn, "Considering the Septuagint."

[26] Jones, "Notes on the Septuagint."

[27] Jobes and Silva, *Introduction to the Septuagint*, consider this topic in great detail.

factors, it is evident that the LXX likely has a place in contributing to our understanding of the Old Testament.

B. Highly Qualified Translators

There is little question but that the translators of the LXX were highly qualified Jewish scholars and rabbis. Certainly this is true for the Torah and likely for the rest of the Old Testament as well.[28] Indeed, so few people knew written Hebrew that the translations were probably done by well-trained Jewish scholars and rabbis as few others would be able to undertake the task. A sizeable number of translators were also likely involved, and this avoided the possible biases of one or two persons. Further, even if one accepts only a fraction of the assertions in the *Letter of Aristeas*, the translators worked under optimal circumstances. Finally, there is the suggestion that the Jewish translators may well have compared their translations and carefully worked out differences between them in an intellectually honest manner.[29] Such a high level of scholarship and collegiality is consistent with what I have often seen in Jewish works today where carefulness, thoroughness, and much discussion prevail before even small decisions are made.

C. Early Recognition

There is universal agreement that the LXX, rather than the Hebrew text, was the version of the Old Testament used by the early church. The huge significance of this point should not be overlooked as it was the Lord himself and the apostles who worked to put the foundations of that church in place. In addition, the authority of the LXX was explicitly recognized very early by a number of theologians. These included the Hellenistic Jewish philosopher Philo[30] as well as a series of early church fathers including Justin Martyr, Irenaeus of Lyons, Cyril of Jerusalem, and

---

[28] For a contrary viewpoint, see the Introduction of *Septuagint Version of the Old Testament* (Grand Rapids: Zondervan, 1977).

[29] *Letter of Aristeas*, verse 302.

[30] Philo's dates were especially early (c20 BCE – c50 CE). His recognition of the LXX is evident in his complete works accessed April, 2021 at http://www.earlyjewishwritings.com/philo.html.

Augustine of Hippo, many of whom considered the LXX to be "inspired."[31] Beyond the endorsement of single individuals, early versions of the Old Testament made by certain Christian groups endorsed the LXX over the Hebrew text including the Old Latin, Slavonic, Syriac, Old Armenian, Old Georgian, and Coptic assemblies.[32]

While the early (pre-Latin) church unquestionably endorsed the LXX, it is necessary to point out that at the time of the Protestant Reformation, the reformers did not embrace the LXX text at all. For example, the writers of *The Westminster Confession of Faith* explicitly endorsed the Hebrew (Masoretic) text and made no room for the LXX.[33] Other confessions took similar positions and consequently, our Old Testament translations today are routinely based on the Hebrew Masoretic text. What is ironic, however, is that none of these confessions adopted the book order and organization of the Hebrew Scriptures. Rather, all of them embraced the LXX organization of the Old Testament including the Westminster Confession.[34] *The irony here is that on the one hand these confessions rejected the LXX in favor of the Hebrew Scriptures while on the other hand they refused to accept the organization of the Hebrew Scriptures and instead imposed on them the organization of the LXX.* The significance of the last sentence is substantial with far-reaching ramifications. However, I have not seen anyone in the Reformed tradition either recognize this incongruity or attempt to resolve it. I do hope that this has been done somewhere and that I have merely missed it.

We cannot go on without addressing the reasons why the reformers distanced themselves from the text of the LXX. It is possible that many Reformed theologians may not have been aware of the outstanding merits of the LXX, and they may not have given it due attention in significant part because the LXX was associated with Catholicism from which they certainly wished to distance themselves. Catholicism was the largest and most notable outgrowth of the early church, and quite early it had gone in the direction of Latin as the language of the people. Indeed, prior to Jerome, the translations of the Old Testament into Latin were regularly

---

[31] Martini, *"Is the Septuagint a Divinely Inspired Translation?"*

[32] Jones, *"Notes on the Septuagint."*

[33] *Westminster Confession of Faith* (1647), Chapter I, Section 8.

[34] *Westminster Confession of Faith* (1647), Chapter I, Section 2.

done based on the LXX. Jerome provided a departure from this because he went out of his way to learn Hebrew, and his *Vulgate* is based on the Hebrew.[35] Nevertheless, the Catholic Church continued to be associated with the LXX at least up to 1517 as is shown by the completion of the *Complutensian Polyglot Bible* in Spain. This interlinear Bible included the LXX above the Latin and its publication was delayed until Pope Leo X sanctioned it in 1520.[36] The delay of publication of this major work clearly shows the association of the LXX with Catholicism at least up to that time.

There is available a detailed summary of the Reformed position regard the LXX.[37] While this summary may not be representative of all viewpoints within the Reformed tradition, it does deal with some of the most relevant issues at hand, and thus it will be reviewed here. This document begins with a clear-cut admission that reformers of the sixteenth and seventeenth centuries spent a great deal of time attempting to refute the claims of Roman theologians who, of course, embraced the LXX. It then focuses upon the question of why it is that most of the quotations of the Old Testament in the New Testament do not use the Hebrew but rather the LXX. In response, the following points were offered: 1) only the words of the Hebrew, "…being immediately inspired by God, and by his singular care providence kept pure in all ages, are therefore authentic" (Westminster Confession of Faith 1:8); 2) the Apostles used the LXX because it was familiar to their audiences, readily available, and because they did not wish to undercut beliefs already in place; 3) the use of the LXX by the Apostles does not mean that they believed it to be inspired; 4) the use of the LXX was permitted because it conveyed the general sense of the Hebrew and not because specific words were quoted; and, 5) the LXX may not be used to correct the Hebrew.

The validity of the assertions in the last paragraph can be questioned, some on the basis of logic and others on the basis of fact. Equally important are several omissions from the list including the following: 1) Jesus (not just the Apostles) quoted the LXX; 2) many quotations of the LXX in the

---

[35] Jobes and Silva, *Invitation to the Septuagint*, 60.

[36] An excellent article on this Bible was accessed in April, 2021 at https://en.wikipedia.org/wiki/Complutensian_Polyglot_Bible.

[37] Purely Presbyterian, accessed April, 2021: https://purelypresbyterian.com/2020/09/07/did-the-apostles-favor-the-septuagint/.

New Testament are nearly word for word; 3) the Reformers themselves abandoned the original organization of the Hebrew scriptures and embraced the LXX organization; 4) it is beyond dispute that the LXX was the Bible of the early church; and, 5) it is difficult to claim that the New Testament is inspired if the LXX is not inspired, since hundreds of verses in the New Testament are from the LXX. These key points are dealt with elsewhere in this chapter.

Truly interesting is the speculation as to what the outcome would have been had the reformers put aside the association of the LXX with the Roman Catholic Church. If so, they might have gone with the LXX instead of the Hebrew and if so, our Old Testament translations today would have been based on the LXX. Had that been the case, it would have been easier for Christians through the centuries to have seen Christ in the Old Testament just as was true for the early church. Indeed, as will be shown in the next section, *christos* appears 38 times in the LXX and thus it was easy for the early church to find Christ there. However, no place in the Hebrew text is there a similar sounding word, and this likely makes it more difficult for us to find the second person of the Trinity in the Old Testament. In short, if the LXX had been accepted by the reformers, our theology could have been impacted, and seeing Christ in the Old Testament by Christians may have been much more common today than is the case. It is hoped that these assertions are provocative enough that they will promote detailed scholarly studies in this area.

D. Correction and Clarification of the Hebrew Text

Not surprisingly, there are uncertainties in the Hebrew text in places, and when these have been encountered, many translators have been willing to turn to the LXX in search of clarification, and in so doing have disregarded the position of the Reformers. In some translations of the Bible, you can find evidence for this in the footnotes where particular words in the LXX are supplied when Hebrew word meanings are uncertain. Also, the pronunciations of words and especially names have been difficult to preserve over the centuries in Hebrew simply because beginning with ancient times, none of the Hebrew letters were recognized as vowels.[38] Greek, on the other hand, has vowels and the pronunciation of Greek words is much better established as the Greek of the era was spoken for centuries in many countries. Thus, by looking at the names in Greek, one can obtain hints as to how those names were originally pronounced in Hebrew. The position supported in the present book is that while the Hebrew can be retained as the primary basis for the Old Testament, it is entirely defensible to put the Masoretic Hebrew text and the LXX side by side in textual studies. It is further believed that difficult passages can be best elucidated by so doing, and this will be demonstrated in our chapter on the Old Testament.

2. The LXX Has Led to the Names We Use for the Second Person of the Trinity

Have you ever wondered where "Jesus" and "Christ" come from? Neither one appears in the Old Testament Hebrew text, and instead, both come from the LXX. In consideration of this matter, it

> **2. LXX—Names Used for the Second Person of the Trinity**
> A. Jesus
> B. Christ

is useful to know that when going from one language to the next, *translate* means to supply a word or words in the second language with a *similar meaning* to those in the first language. In contrast, *transliterate* means to supply letters and words in the second language which have *similar sounds* as the words in the first language. Both of these techniques are used by language translators and both are important here.

A. Jesus

Let us see how the name "Jesus" came down to us beginning with the Hebrew. *Yhowshuwa* is a Hebrew name in the Old Testament and this name means "Jehovah saves." When this was transliterated from the Hebrew into English, "Joshua" resulted and this name was the name of the man who is most featured in the Old Testament book that bears his English name. The very same Hebrew name is also the basis for the name

---

[38] Steven E. Fassberg, "Languages of the Bible," in Adele Berlin, and Marc Zvi Brettler, eds., *The Jewish Study Bible* (New York: Oxford University Press, 2004), 1667, 2062–67.

Jesus, but this name could not have come to us directly from the Hebrew as it once again would have been rendered as "Joshua." Instead, when it was transliterated into Greek in the LXX, it was rendered *Iesous* and when that word was transliterated into English, it became "Jesus." Thus, we got the name "Jesus" by going through the LXX and this name is clearly different in our English Bibles from "Joshua." This is true even though both names came from exactly the same Hebrew word. They were, after all, two separate people. In summary, by going through the Greek, two names emerge in English translations for two people (Joshua, Jesus) from the Hebrew *Yhowshuwa,* whereas if one went directly from the Hebrew to the English this would not have been possible. Thus, the LXX provided a vital link in giving us the name Jesus. A truly interesting in-depth discussion of the origin of the English words "Joshua" and "Jesus" is given by Charles Van der Pool.[39]

B. Christ

In the Hebrew Old Testament, the word *mashiyach* appears and when translated into English, it is most commonly rendered "anointed one." When it is transliterated from the Hebrew into English, "Messiah" is often rendered which gives a similar sound to the Hebrew *mashiyach.* You can refer to passages such as Daniel 9:25–26 in your favorite Old Testament translation to see whether your version used translation or transliteration. However, the major point here is that neither of these approaches gets us even close to "Christ," which is where we need to get in order to portray Jesus as truly anointed by God (Acts 10:38).

To convey the meaning of *mashiyach* in Greek, the LXX translated this Hebrew word into *chrio* which in Greek means to rub ceremoniously with oil. This, in fact, is what happened to priests and kings when they assumed their offices—they were anointed with oil. When a noun form of the verb *chrio* was called for (such as when a specific person was named), that noun form was *christos.* Therefore, the translators of the LXX commonly used *christos* when they found *mashiyach* in the Hebrew text. Later, when the English translations were made from the Greek, the *christos* in Greek was

---

[39] Van der Pool, Charles. "Introduction to the Book of Joshua" video, 2021, accessed April, 2021 at https://www.youtube.com/watch?v=VmbffvsbOuw&feature=youtu.be.

routinely transliterated into "Christ." As you can see, there is no way that one can get to "Christ" from the Hebrew scriptures except through the LXX, and this is exactly how we got a primary title for our Savior. Further, if you call yourself a "Christian," that is how you got that name—through the LXX!

The gravity of the material in the last paragraph will become even more evident by looking at a few Old Testament passages. First, consider Psalm 2:1–2 and note how verse 2 ends. In nearly every English translation the verse ends in "anointed" or "anointed one," and this is because our Old Testament translations follows the Hebrew text primarily. However, the LXX does not conclude

> **Psalm 2:1–2**
>
> Why do the nations conspire and the peoples plot in vain? The kings of the earth rise up and the rulers band together against the Lord and against his anointed.

verse 2 in this way but rather in *christos,* and if your English translation was following the LXX, it would have the word "Christ" in the text at the end of verse 2. That removes any uncertainty as to whom "his anointed" refers, and if you have any doubt as to whether this is correct, turn to Acts 4:23–27 where this psalm is quoted and where with absolute certainty it means Jesus Christ. Thus, the LXX points us towards this conclusion but the Hebrew does not.

Continuing in the same mode, consider Psalm 132:10–17 and look in particular at the last words of verses 10 and 17. As before, you will very likely find "anointed" or "anointed one" in your Bible, but again the LXX inserts *christos.* As you look at the psalm itself, you will likely conclude that it has an immediate application to King David but that it also is a Messianic psalm. As such, it is nice that the insertion of *christos* in such psalms helps to explain what we already know. Actually, however, the chronological order is just the

> **Psalm 132:10 & 17**
>
> 10. For the sake of your servant David, do not reject your anointed one (*christos*).
>
> 17. "Here I will make a horn grow for David and set up a lamp for my anointed one (*christos*)."

opposite, because in the LXX, *christos* was inserted in the psalms and elsewhere in the Old Testament many years before Jesus was born. While it is clear that the use of *christos* by the LXX refers to Christ in various places in the Old Testament, note is made that it is also occasionally used in connection with other people, the most common being Samuel. Altogether, the word appears 38 times in the LXX.[40]

The thrust of all of this is that the LXX set the stage for the use of "Christ" in the New Testament, and without the LXX, one can debate whether Jesus would ever have been called "Christ." Early Christians were very willing to use the title "Christ" and indeed its first use in Greek was in Matthew 1:1! This immediate identification of Jesus as the Christ was the first of more than 500 uses of *christos* in the New Testament, and the use of that same term in the Old Testament must have made it easy for people in the early church to find him there. The Jewish religious leaders also knew the term, and the Greek New Testament shows that it was used by the high priest at the trial of Jesus (Matthew 26:63), and by the Jewish rulers while Jesus was on the cross (Luke 23:35).

Not only did religious people know the term "Christ," but secular people did as well. In Matthew 2:3–4, for example, the Greek New Testament tells us that King Herod called the Jewish leaders together and asked them where "the Christ" was to be born. How did he know about "the Christ"? And how about Pilate who again in the Greek New Testament used "Christ" while examining Jesus before his crucifixion (Matthew 27:17 & 22)? How did he become familiar with the term? One can only conclude that the term had to be in reasonably common usage for these men to know it, and the common usage of the term in Greek can be reasonably attributed only to the LXX. Indeed, there is no similar sounding word in the Hebrew, and it is clear that it is much easier to find Christ in the Greek LXX.

PAUSE

At this point it would be worth pausing and asking where we would be with regard to the very names of our Savior without the LXX. What

---

[40] The 38 scriptures in which *christos* appears in the LXX are as follows: Leviticus 4:5 & 16, 6:22, 21:10 & 12; 1 Samuel 2:10 & 35, 12:3 & 5, 16:6, 24:6 & 10, 26:9, 11, 16, & 23; 2 Samuel 1:14 & 16, 19:21, 22:51, 23:1; 1 Chronicles 16:22; 2 Chronicles 6:42, 22:7; Psalms 2:2, 18:50, 20:6, 28:8, 84:9, 89:38 & 51, 105:15, 132:10 & 17; Isaiah 45:1; Lamentations 4:20; Daniel 9:25; Habakkuk 3:13.

would the New Testament look like if the words "Jesus" and "Christ" were nowhere to be found?

---

3. The LXX Reorganized the Books in the Hebrew Bible

Earlier, reference was made to the fact that the LXX reorganized the Hebrew Old Testament, and that this reorganization has been broadly accepted, including by the Reformers. As a consequence, the order of the books in the Old Testament in our Bible does not follow the order of the Hebrew text but rather the order established by the LXX. See how the two orders contrast with one another in table 3. Even a glance at this table shows significant changes by the LXX. The order of the books is changed, some of the Hebrew books are divided into two books, and the 12 Minor Prophets are no longer grouped as one, but each is a separate book.

> **3. LXX—Reorganized the Hebrew Bible**
> A. Human explanations
>   i. Existing order not entirely logical
>   ii. Some books exceptionally long
>   iii. Book of Daniel
> B. Benefits for Christians
>   i. Clear teaching of life after death
>   ii. All scriptures of equal importance
>   iii. Timing of translation

As already discussed, it is extremely likely indeed that Jewish scholars and rabbis did the LXX translation, and the irony here is that they made substantial changes in the organization of the Old Testament. Surely, most Jewish scholars would not reorganize the Hebrew Scriptures either then or now. It would be like one of us, in making a translation of the New Testament, decided to move the books all around because we liked a certain new order better such as arranging the books alphabetically by book title, splitting Romans into two pieces because we thought it was too long, etc. As we will see, the Old Testament reorganization has had a substantial impact on how Christians view scripture today. Therefore, we will first examine possible human reasons for the reorganization, and then offer a divine explanation.

Table 3. Comparison of Old Testament book arrangements		
Hebrew Bible—24 books	Septuagint (LXX)—39 books	LXX Common Grouping
Law (Torah)	Genesis	
Genesis	Exodus	
Exodus	Leviticus	**Law**
Leviticus	Numbers	
Numbers	Deuteronomy	
Deuteronomy	Joshua	
	Judges	
Prophets (Nevi'im)	Ruth	
Joshua	1 Samuel	
Judges	2 Samuel	
Samuel	1 Kings	
Kings	2 Kings	**History**
Isaiah	1 Chronicles	
Jeremiah	2 Chronicles	
Ezekiel	Ezra	
The Twelve (minor prophets)	Nehemiah	
	Esther	
Writings (Ketuvim)	Job	
Psalms	Psalms	
Proverbs	Proverbs	**Writings/Poetry**
Job	Ecclesiastes	
Song of Songs	Song of Solomon	
Ruth	Isaiah	
Lamentations	Jeremiah	
Ecclesiastes	Lamentations	**Major Prophets**
Esther	Ezekiel	
Daniel	Daniel	
Ezra-Nehemiah	Hosea	
Chronicles	Joel	
	Amos	
	Obadiah	
	Jonah	
	Micah	
	Nahum	**Minor Prophets**
	Habakkuk	
	Zephaniah	
	Haggai	
	Zechariah	
	Malachi	

A. Human Explanations for the Reorganization

There are at least three human explanations for the reorganization:

i. The order of the books in the Hebrew text was not entirely logical. The order of books in the Hebrew Bible had evolved over time, and in view of the well-established emphasis in Greek thinking on organization and logic, the translators may have made changes to make the organization of the overall document to appear more logical and therefore more acceptable to a Greek-speaking audience. For example, in the Hebrew Bible, the history of the Jewish people is spread from one end of the Old Testament to the other end with other kinds of writings interspersed in various places. Some of the historical accounts are also out of order such as Chronicles being at the very end of the Bible but recounting the early history of the United Kingdom. Ezra-Nehemiah is placed before Chronicles even though it actually occurred after Chronicles and is a continuation of it.[41]

Other irregularities in book order are evident. Jeremiah and Lamentations are far apart in the Hebrew Bible while they deal with the same period of Jewish history and they likely have the same author (Jeremiah). And by the way, should the judges and the kings really be grouped with the prophets as the judges and the kings were not prophets in the commonly used sense of the term? It would be more logical to put the prophetical books together. Overall, quite a few concerns with regard to book ordering and organization had accumulated. The translators may have concluded that it only made sense to straighten out all these problems at this key point in time when their sacred scripture was being introduced to the Greek-speaking world in its own language.

ii. Some books were exceptionally long, making them less readable. The historical books of Samuel, Kings and Chronicles were all very long and each was quite easily split into two pieces. Having the twelve Minor Prophets each stand on their own as separate books instead of as one long book made logical sense for the uninitiated reader, and especially so as the themes and contents of the books were different. Therefore, "The Twelve" was divided into twelve books. Finally, it may have simply made sense

---

[41] Berlin and Brettler, *Jewish Study Bible*, 1712-17.

to separate Ezra and Nehemiah because the content of the two books is significantly different even though the two men lived during the same era. Besides, it may have seemed odd to have a book having two names in the title when all the other books with names in their titles had just one name.

iii. Dealing with the book of Daniel was especially important. Daniel appeared to be a prophet, but his book had been placed far away from the prophets in the Hebrew text, and a major move was required. The translators may very well have believed that he was a prophet and that therefore his book should be put among the prophets and they did just that.

The placement of Daniel does not seem like a big deal to Christians today, but to the Jews, classifying Daniel was (and still is) a problem. While there is evidence that early Jewish thinkers (likely including the translators of the LXX) did identify him as a prophet as shown in the Dead Sea Scrolls, there were problems in so doing.[42] For example, nowhere in Daniel does the phrase, "Thus sayeth the Lord" appear as would be expected with a prophet. The book was also written in two languages, Hebrew and Aramaic which made it suspect—why not all in Hebrew? Then there was its apocalyptic nature which is unparalleled in the Hebrew Scriptures and which was difficult to interpret by the rabbis.

Once Jesus had come, Christians saw in Daniel prefigurations of Jesus as well as some of the teachings of Jesus such as the existence of an afterlife. The rabbis wished to distance Judaism from such beliefs and to maintain its distinction from Christianity. Given all these factors, rabbinical Judaism over the centuries has declined to call Daniel a prophet, but rather a *seer*, which implies the ability to foretell the future without giving him the status of a prophet.[43] However, and in the end, the translators of the LXX not only called Daniel a prophet but they placed his book among the most important prophets in the Old Testament. This is truly remarkable as it is a clear departure from the Jewish thought that had put the book of Daniel near the end of the Old Testament originally and which has kept that placement ever since.

The three reasons just given for the reorganization of the LXX by its

---

[42] Berlin and Brettler, *Jewish Study Bible,* 1642.
[43] Berlin and Brettler, *Jewish Study Bible,* 1640-1642.

translators are human explanations for why the Jewish scholars and rabbis might have been willing to reorganize the Hebrew Scriptures as they did. However, these human explanations ignore the fact that it is most unlikely that devout Jews either then or now would ever tamper with either the text or the organization of their Bible. Why, then, were those changes made? One cannot escape the possibility that the reason may be because God wanted the Old Testament reorganized and he merely used the LXX translators to achieve that end. This, then, is a *divine explanation*. There may have been objectives which God wanted to achieve so that the Old Testament would be more tightly connected with the New Testament and of greater value and usefulness to the Christians who would be on the scene before long. These goals could actually be met without changing a word of the text itself but merely by changing the organization of the books.

B. Benefits of the Reorganization for Christians

The reorganization had at least three major benefits for Christians:

i. The presence of a clear teaching of life after death. With the original organization of the Hebrew text, it was not at all clear that the Old Testament teaches that there is life after death. At the time of Christ, this issue sharply divided the Pharisees and the Sadducees. The former believed in the resurrection of the dead and the latter basically said, "Where is it written?" to which the Pharisees did not have a good answer. The continuing uncertainties in Jewish circles even today about whether there is life after death were well reflected by one of my Jewish friends who, when asked if he believed in life after death, simply said, "We hope so."

Daniel's prophecies clearly point to life after death but if you do not believe that Daniel was a prophet but only a "seer" or someone similar, the most convincing evidence for life after death in the Old Testament dissipates. However, when the book of Daniel is placed not just among the prophets but among the most important of the prophets (commonly called Major Prophets), the Old Testament teaching of life after death is greatly strengthened. And placement of Daniel with the other prophets is certainly appropriate because Jesus plainly said that he was a prophet (Matthew 24:15). Overall, a divine motive can be seen not only in the change in the position of Daniel in the canon to be with the other prophets, but also in pointing to an answer to the life after death question which is in harmony with many teachings in the New Testament.

ii. Abandonment of different levels of importance of particular sections of scripture. It is absolutely the case that the law (Torah) is identified as the most important section of the Hebrew Scriptures by Jews today. Further, the prophets (Nevi'im) are of intermediate importance, and that the writings (Ketuvim) are of least importance. That is also the order in which they are placed in the Hebrew Bible. If you talk with Jewish people, they will clearly affirm this hierarchy with the law at the top in terms of importance and the writings at the bottom. It is likely indeed that the order of the books has promoted this hierarchy.

As Christians, we need to ask whether God wants us to view the scriptures with the outlook that some are not as important as others. The vast majority of Christians believe that this is not the case and that instead God wants us to view ALL scripture as inspired and of importance. Not only does the order of the books in the LXX not promote a ranking by importance, but *the LXX order actually makes it impossible to rank the books by presumed importance.* For example, Ruth comes well before Isaiah, but it is impossible to say that Ruth is more

> **2 Timothy 3:16**
> All scripture is God-breathed and is useful for teaching, rebuking, correcting and training in righteousness.

important than Isaiah. Likewise, Esther comes before Psalms but you cannot therefore say that Esther has a higher status. Ruth and Esther are both important, but you cannot use the order in which they appear to establish the degree of their importance. Thus, the principle to which the LXX has drawn us is the same as what we find in the New Testament, namely, that all scripture is inspired by God and is therefore important.

iii. The timing of the LXX translation. It is worth noting that the reorganization of the Old Testament books by the LXX was done in time for that reorganization to be firmly established before the very first convert to Christianity. The reorganization has held through the centuries with essentially every non-Jewish Old Testament Bible translation done since the time of Christ showing the LXX organization. It is reasonable to presume that this must have been the intention of the Almighty because the LXX organization of the Old Testament is the only organization that the typical Christian has ever seen.

4. The LXX was Broadly Influential for Centuries

Let us now go on to the fourth outstanding feature of the LXX, and this pertains to the fact that it was highly influential for hundreds of years after its translation. In connection with this influence, three groups of people deserve special comment:

> **4. LXX—Influential for Centuries**
> A. Jews
> B. General secular population
> C. Christians

A. Jews

At the time the LXX was translated, the Jews were spread out widely and many could no longer speak Hebrew but rather the prevalent language of the day, Greek. To teach a child Hebrew to the point that the scriptures could be read would be an extremely difficult task that few parents would even attempt and that is true even now. Hebrew is a difficult language to learn for a number or reasons. The letters have unique shapes and the words are difficult to pronounce as there is not a typical presentation of vowel sounds. In order to pronounce the words, you must know which vowel sounds need to be inserted in the syllables of every word, something which takes a very substantial amount of training. Further, reading from right to left is especially difficult when most native languages (like Greek) go in the other direction. It is no wonder that knowledge of Hebrew was limited and especially so outside Israel.

With the mastering of Hebrew being such a daunting task, you can imagine the relief that many Jews must have felt when their scriptures were finally available in a language they understood and used every day. Furthermore, it was translated not by gentiles but by very able Jewish scholars and rabbis so it had credibility among Jews from the start. The influence of the LXX among Jews continued for perhaps 300 years after its translation and probably until sometime after Jesus died on the cross. By then, Christians had embraced the LXX so warmly that the Jews distanced themselves from it. Therefore, and under rabbinical influence,

Judaism moved away from the LXX and back to what they believed (and still believe) was the superior Hebrew text.[44]

B. General Secular Population

The substantial effort that was made to translate the Hebrew Bible into Greek, plus its celebrated welcome into the most famous library in the world, must have resulted in a remarkable amount of attention being paid to the LXX. With information about Judaism now readily available to people who were not Jewish, a number of gentiles became interested in Judaism as is shown in the New Testament. For example, John 12:20–21 tells us that there were some Greeks who went to Jerusalem to worship at the Jewish feast. In the book of Acts, the travels of the Apostles are recorded and it is noted that on a number of occasions they found gentiles who were God-fearing and connected to Judaism (see Acts 14:1 and 17:4). It is exceedingly probable that most or all of these people were informed about Judaism through the LXX. It has already been pointed out how even non-Christian people were familiar with the term "Christ" during the life of Jesus. Overall, it appears likely indeed that, using the well-known Greek language, the LXX had an impact upon the general population.

> **John 12:20–21**
>
> Now there were some Greeks among those who went up to worship at the festival. They came to Philip, who was from Bethsaida in Galilee, with a request. "Sir," they said, "we would like to see Jesus."

C. Christians

After the death of Jesus, Christians embraced the LXX and it unquestionably became the Bible of the New Testament church. Christians of the era could not miss seeing Christ in the Old Testament because from their viewpoint, his very name appeared there. Indeed, as already shown, his name came from the LXX. The prophecies of the coming of the Messiah made sense to them in the person of Jesus. Further, the foreshadowings of him in the

---

[44] Berlin and Brettler, *Jewish Study Bible,* 2006-08.

Old Testament were reinforced by many people who had witnessed Christ in person or who knew those who had.

The adoption of the LXX by early Christians is emphatically underscored in the New Testament where passages from the Old Testament are referenced or quoted. Theologians seem to agree that there are at least 200 of these passages and some say more than 300 (some may be allusions to Old Testament passages rather than direct quotes of them). The scholar who has perhaps dealt the most extensively with this and related issues is R. Grant Jones who was referenced previously.[45] In a major paper, he studied a number of matters pertaining to the LXX including quotes of it in the New Testament. In connection with those quotes, he compared the LXX with the Hebrew text in a detailed way. In general, his work and that of others show that the New Testament Greek agrees with the LXX definitely more frequently than it does with the Hebrew text.[46] The implication is that the New Testament speakers and writers much more often quoted the LXX than the Hebrew. Indeed, preference for the LXX over the Hebrew by New Testament writers may be as high as nine times out of 10.[47] Quotations of the LXX were especially common by the Apostle Paul, but they are found by most other New Testament writers and speakers including Jesus.

We will now illustrate what has just been said by examining a quote by Jesus of a passage in Isaiah as recorded in the gospels. In Matthew 13, Jesus responds to a question of the disciples as to why he spoke to the people in parables. In his response, he quoted Isaiah 6:9–10. This is the passage in which Isaiah was commissioned to take the message of the Lord to the people, and Isaiah volunteers to do just that. However, Isaiah is warned that even though the people will have heard and seen the truth, they will not really understand it nor take it to heart.

Let us first look at the Greek New Testament passage which is presented in the text box in interlinear format. In this format, a word by word English translation is presented below the corresponding words in Greek.[48] Above the Greek words are numbers from the Strong numbering

[45] Jones, *"Notes on the Septuagint."*

[46] Jobes and Silva, *Invitation to the Septuagint*, 207-08.

[47] Martini, *"Is the Septuagint a Divinely Inspired Translation?"*

[48] Greek/English interlinear selections taken from Charles Van der Pool, *The Apostolic Bible Polyglot* (Newport OR: Apostolic Press, 1996). Used by permission.

system,[49] in which each of the 5,624 Greek words in the New Testament has been given a different number. Using this setup, you can get a good idea of what was said, even if you do not know a word of Greek.

Now look at the next text box which gives the original passage from Isaiah 6:9–10 as recorded in the LXX. You can compare the English word for word and you can also compare the Greek words using the numbering system. If you compare the Greek words, you will find that the words are exactly the same except that in the Matthew account it is "the ears" and "the eyes" whereas in Isaiah it is "their ears" and "their eyes." Thus, with the slightest differences, Jesus has quoted the LXX word for word.

Matthew 13:14–15

		189	191	2532
		ακοη	ακουσετε	και
		Hearing	you shall hear,	and

3766.2	4920		2532 991	991	2532
ου μη	συνητε		και βλεποντες	βλεψετε	και
in no way	should you perceive;		and seeing	you shall see,	and

3766.2	1492		3975		1063 3588 2588
ου μη	ιδητε	13:15 επαχυνθη		γαρ η	καρδια
in no way should you know.		[⁵was thickened		¹For ²the	³heart

3588 2992-3778		2532 3588	3775 917	191	2532
του λαου τουτου		και τοις	ωσι βαρεως	ηκουσαν	και
⁴of this people],		and with the	ears heavily	they heard,	and

3588 3788-1473		2576		3379
τους οφθαλμους αυτων	εκαμμυσαν			μηποτε
[²of their eyes	¹they closed the eyelids]:			lest at any time

1492		3588	3788	2532 3588	3775 191
ιδωσι		τοις	οφθαλμοις και τοις		ωσιν ακουσωσιν
they should see		with the eyes,		and with the ears	should hear,

2532 3588 2588	4920		2532	1994	2532
και τη καρδια	συνωσι		και	επιστρεψωσι	και
and the heart	should perceive,		and	they should turn,	and

| 2390 | 1473 |
| ιασομαι | αυτους |
| I shall heal them. |

It is fair to ask what the Hebrew is for the same passage in Isaiah, and while the overall meaning of it is very much the same, there are definitely differences. For example, "people" are referred to at the beginning but "him" at the end. This plural vs. singular difference is of uncertain

---

[49] James Strong, *Strong's Exhaustive Concordance* (Nashville: Crusade Bible Publishers, 1960). First published in 1890.

significance. At the end, who does the healing does seem to be different, and the broadly accepted Jewish *Tanakh* translation says, "And repent and save itself."[50] It seems unlikely indeed that Jesus would have chosen to have the passage end in this way. Overall, it is evident that the New Testament Greek agrees with the LXX but disagrees in notable ways with the Masoretic Hebrew text.[51]

Isaiah 6:9–10

	189	*191*	*2532 3766.2*
	ακοή	ακούσετε	και ου μη
	Hearing,	you shall hear,	but in no way

4920	*2532 991*	*991*	*2532 3766.2*
συνείτε	και βλέποντες	βλέψετε	και ου μη
shall you perceive;	and seeing	you shall see,	but in no way

1492	*3975*	*1063 3588*	*2588 3588*
ίδητε	6:10 επαχύνθη	γαρ ή	καρδία του
shall you know.	[⁵was thickened	¹For ²the	³heart

2992-3778	*2532 3588 3775-1473*	*917 191*	*2532*
λαού τούτου	και τοις ωσίν αυτών	βαρέως ήκουσαν	και
⁴of this people]; and	[³with their ears	²heavily ¹they heard], and	

3588 3788	*2576*	*3379*	*1492*
τους οφθαλμούς	εκάμμυσαν	μήποτε	ίδωσι
the eyes	closed eyelids.	lest at any time	they should behold

3588 3788-1473	*2532 3588 3775*	*191*	*2532 3588*
τοις οφθαλμοίς αυτών	και τοις ωσίν	ακούσωσι	και τη
with their eyes,	and the ears	should hear,	and the

2588 4920	*2532 1994*	*2532 2390*	
καρδία συνώσι	και επιστρέψωσι	και ιάσομαι	
heart should perceive,	and they should turn,	and I shall heal	

| *1473* |
| αυτούς |
| them. |

The evidence presented here is compelling that Jesus quoted the LXX over the Hebrew, and one can only conclude that significant credence is added to the validity of the LXX. It should also be noted that the Apostle Paul routinely quoted the LXX in the huge number of Old Testament citations he made, and frequently word for word. Again this is notable since as a devout Pharisee, he obviously knew Hebrew very well indeed but chose to quote the Greek.

---

[50] Berlin and Brettler, *Jewish Study Bible*, 797.
[51] Robert H. Gundry, *Matthew: A Commentary on His Handbook for a Mixed Church Under Persecution*, 2nd ed. (Grand Rapids: William B. Eerdmans, 1994), 257.

5. The LXX Provided the Names We Use Today for God in the Entire Bible

This is the fifth and final major area of LXX influence which we will discuss. Multiple names and titles for God exist in the Hebrew Old Testament with some people even believing that there are as many as 72![52] However, if you limit yourself to actual names of God and not to divine attributes, you might conclude that there are about a dozen.

> **5. LXX—Provided Names for God**
> A. In the Old Testament
> B. In the New Testament

Alfred Norris lists 12 names for God and gives them and the frequencies that they occur in the Old Testament as follows: Yahweh 6,807; Elohim 2,340; Adonai 428; Sabaoth 278; El 221; Elahh 74; Eloah 52; Shaddai 48; Yah 40; Elyon 35; Adon 27; Illay 9.[53] Note that none of these names deal with the Holy Spirit as the Jews do not conceive of a separately identified person of the Trinity with characteristics which Christians ascribe to the Holy Spirit. This need not be of great concern to us as we typically do not have much difficulty in identifying the Holy Spirit in the Old Testament. For example, in 50 or more cases "Spirit of God" or "Spirit of the Lord" are found which most Christians would agree refers to the Holy Spirit with little or no discussion.

The difficulty is in sorting out the work of the first and second persons of the Trinity in the Old Testament when given a dozen names for God. Which names usually or always refer to the first person of the Trinity and which names usually or always refer to the second? Or, can one name refer to both persons at the same time? Answering these questions is difficult, but the reality is this: *unless we can at least reasonably well sort out these names with regard to the first and second persons of the Trinity, we will not have any consistent success in finding the person and work of Jesus in the Old Testament.*

Probably unintentionally, the translators of the LXX gave us major assistance in dealing with the task at hand by boiling down all 12 names

---

[52] Position held by Kabbalah, a mystical brand of Judaism. Holly Nelson-Becker, *Spirituality, Religion, and Aging* (Los Angeles: Sage, 2018), 255.

[53] Alfred Norris, *What Is His Name? A Biblical Study of Divine Titles* (Aletheia Books, 1986).

for God to just two: God (*Theos*) and Lord (*Kurios*). In general, *Kurios* means **Lord** and it was used when Yahweh and Adonai were encountered in the Hebrew. In general also, *Theos* means **God** and it was used in Greek when all the other 10 names appeared in Hebrew. The translators could have used transliteration to include some of the Hebrew names for God in the Greek text, but they did not include a single Hebrew name in the LXX. This is truly remarkable and even more so because many of those Hebrew names had been given particular meanings by the Jews over the centuries. Therefore, those shades of meaning were lost when the names were dropped. Why did these Jewish scholars drop these names, and could this have been part of a divine plan?

The matter at hand is even more remarkable when it is realized that the New Testament writers uniformly followed the LXX with regard to the names for God. They also dropped all the Hebrew names for God and just used *Kurios* and *Theos*. As a result of their following the practice of the LXX, the words "God" and "Lord" are the persisting and enduring single names for God found in the entire Bible. Worthy of further note is the fact that while the Old Testament in your Bible is based on the Hebrew text, when it comes to the names for God, your Bible follows the LXX by making no effort whatever to transliterate the names for God. Instead, your Bible simply says "God" or "Lord" with only rare exceptions. Again, one wonders if this could be part of a divine plan.

Note that while the general use of "God" and "Lord" does prevail throughout the Bible, there are other variations that do appear in the Old Testament, and they typically use more than one word. They include "Lord God," "God Most High," "God Almighty," "Lord Almighty," and "Lord your God." When these and other names are found in the Old Testament, there is a persistent tendency for them to include "God" or "Lord." In the New Testament, we certainly have "Jesus," "Christ," "Jesus Christ," and "the Father," none of which include "God" or "Lord." Nevertheless, it is easy for "God" or "Lord" to be included in these names, and these two names must be the most commonly used names in the Bible for the first and second persons of the Trinity. Our strategy will be to initially study "God" and "Lord" in the New Testament to see to which members of the Trinity they apply. Once we understand those names more fully in the New Testament, we will be able to take what we have learned to the Old

Testament and see if that information will be helpful in determining which members of the Trinity are at work in given passages there.

6. Criticisms of the LXX

In my experience, the LXX has typically received only brief coverage in most Bible curriculums, and not always with a positive tone. Detailed critiques are available elsewhere[54] but the primary issues that have been raised about the LXX can be dealt with economically under three headings.

A. Details about the History of the Translation

As would certainly be expected for such a very early translation, firmly established details are missing about the translators and the circumstances under which the LXX translation was accomplished. To be sure, the Letter of Aristeas gives this information, but scholars often criticize this letter for various reasons even though they are routinely unable to prove that critical points in it are contrary to established fact. For example, no one can prove that the names of the translators given in the letter are incorrect or that the circumstances under which the translation occurred are in error. We do not demand such information about the Hebrew text from which the LXX was translated, so should we demand this information for the LXX? And consider this: what if 50 years from now someone writes glowing (or negative) comments about the book you are now reading in terms of the circumstances in which it was written? Does that make this book any more (or less) valid? No, certainly not! This book needs to stand on its own merits, as does the LXX, with or without historical contextual information.

B. A Focus upon the Greek Used in the LXX

Scholars can pick at the Greek in the earliest of the LXX fragments including defects in the grammar with the conclusion that it was not translated and recorded by highly educated people. However, the LXX is a very early example of Koine Greek. As is well known, Koine Greek began at the time of Alexander the Great (about 330 BCE), and the development of Koine grammar was at best in progress in about 280 BCE

---

[54] Examples are to be found in the Introduction of *Septuagint Version of the Old Testament* (Grand Rapids: Zondervan, 1977), and in Jobes and Silva, *Introduction to the Septuagint*.

when the translation of the LXX began. By the time of writing of the New Testament, that form of the Greek language was well established and polished. But it is unrealistic to expect such polish at the time of the LXX, and it may also not have helped that the translation of the LXX was done far from Greece itself. These factors need to be taken into account in evaluating the Greek of the LXX.

C. Defects in the Translation Itself

While the Torah and other parts of the LXX have received little criticism, there are some difficulties in the LXX translation of some of the prophets.[55] I believe that this is the greatest criticism of the LXX that has been offered and I do not discount this criticism. However, I would point out that none of us have at hand the Hebrew manuscripts from which the LXX translation was made. I refer not to the polished Masoretic manuscripts of the ninth century CE, but to the Hebrew manuscripts of the third century BCE. Indeed, there may have been significant limitations in the particular copies of early Hebrew manuscripts available to the LXX translators, but we simply do not know.

The above is intended only to hit the high points of some of the criticisms that have been offered of the LXX. Clearly, it is a translation made by humans and it will have human limitations. However, God can use the work of humans, and it appears that he has done so here and seemingly in very interesting ways.

Conclusions

This complex chapter has focused upon an exploration of the potential contributions of the LXX to discovering Jesus in the Old Testament. I know of no prior published effort to achieve this goal with the LXX. There are merits to some of the criticisms of the LXX, but a focus on them must not keep us from recognizing the following facts:

- The LXX is by far the earliest essentially complete translation that we have of the Old Testament. While based on very early Hebrew

---

[55] See Jobes and Silva, *Introduction to the* Septuagint, 181-199, for a discussion of these especially in regard to the Dead Sea Scrolls.

manuscripts, those are no longer available, and the Masoretic Hebrew text used today was assembled much later.

- There is evidence that the Jews initially accepted the LXX, but early in the Common Era they rejected it, a prime reason likely being because Christians obviously embraced it.

- Without doubt, the LXX was the Bible of the early church, Christ quoted it, and the New Testament writers quoted it far more frequently than the Hebrew text. The nearly exclusive use of it by the Apostle Paul is especially noteworthy. These facts alone put all criticisms of the LXX into a diminished position of importance, and if Christ quoted the LXX repeatedly, what criticism of significance can be found against it?

- The LXX led to the names we most commonly use for the second person of the Trinity, namely, "Jesus" and "Christ."

- "Christ" is much easier to find in the LXX than in the Hebrew because the Hebrew has neither a similar-sounding word or one which is translated as "Christ" in English. This may contribute to the fact that Christians today have difficulty in finding Jesus in the Old Testament as they routinely use translations based upon the Hebrew.

- The LXX reorganized the Hebrew scriptures in a way that has held for essentially all versions of the Old Testament from before Jesus was born in Bethlehem until today. The versions produced by Jews represent the only exceptions to this pervasive rule.

- The LXX has been broadly influential for centuries, but it was rejected by the reformers likely in significant part because it was associated with the Roman Catholic Church.

- Finally, the LXX used "God" and "Lord" as the enduring single names for God, and this now holds true in our Bibles from Genesis to Revelation. These names provide a strong bridge across the testaments, a bridge which will help us to explore our Savior being vibrantly at work in both.

Taken together, these bullet points provide strong evidence that the LXX is at the minimum a viable tool in understanding the Old Testament. Its authority needs to be more broadly recognized, and it is completely reasonable to put it alongside the Hebrew text and to use them together to better understand what is being conveyed.[56]

With the help of the LXX, we have now uncovered the first of three keys which we will use to assist in identifying the person and work of Jesus Christ in the Old Testament. This is **Key #1: Enduring Names for God—"God" and "Lord."** In the next chapter we will study those names in the New Testament, and we will identify two additional keys to help us distinguish between the first and second persons of the Trinity. We will then use all three keys together in our New Testament studies, and only when we have validated them in terms of their ability to distinguish between the first and second persons of the Trinity will we apply them to the Old Testament with the objective of making the same distinction.

---

[56] No side-by-side editions of a standard English translation of the standard Old Testament and the LXX are known to your author. The LXX Old Testament books are available in English interspersed with multiple associated apocryphal writings in Albert Pietersma and Benjamin G. Wright (eds.), *New English Translation of the Septuagint* (New York: Oxford Univ. Press, 2007).

Four

The New Testament: Keys to Identifying the First and Second Persons of the Trinity

In our studies thus far, we have noted the tendency of most Christians to have little or no awareness of the possible involvement of Jesus with people prior to his birth in Bethlehem, and in this book we are being challenged to broaden this viewpoint. To provide important information to meet this challenge, in chapter 2 we reviewed Jewish history with a particular emphasis on the 500 years before Jesus was born. During that time the Old Testament was translated into Greek, and by studying that translation in chapter 3, we found the first key to distinguishing between the first and second persons of the Trinity. This is **Key #1: Enduring Names for God—"God" and "Lord."**

We now continue our studies, and our plan is to begin with the application of our first key in an effort to determine its usefulness in distinguishing between the first and second persons of the Trinity in the New Testament. Then we will go on to find and study two additional keys that have been selected to meet the same goal. Finally, we will evaluate the ability of all three keys working together to meet that end. We are deliberately starting with the New Testament because we already have a good understanding of which members of the Trinity are likely at work in most passages. Also, starting in this way will enable us to become familiar with the keys and to test them out, finding their strengths and any weaknesses that may exist. That will put us in a good position to apply these keys to the Old Testament in the next chapter so that we can better assess to what degree Jesus may be at work there.

Key #1—Enduring Names for God

In the last chapter, we showed that the Septuagint (LXX) boiled down the many Hebrew names for God to two: "God" and "Lord." Furthermore, it was exactly those two names that were carried over to the New Testament by its writers, and *not on even one occasion* did they try to bring in any of the other Hebrew names into the New Testament. As a consequence, "God" and "Lord" are the two enduring single names for God found in the entire Bible. Since these names transcend the Old Testament and the New Testament, they add important unity to the scriptures as a whole. One cannot help but raise the possibility that this is exactly what God wanted, and if so, we would be well advised to set about an intense study of these two names.

1. Studies of "God" in the New Testament

Referring to the divine, the proper noun "God" appears in the NIV New Testament translation we are using (Zondervan, 2011) 1,248 times.[57] The possessive form ("God's") of it appears on 192 occasions for a total of 1,440 occurrences. Not surprisingly, the word "God" is routinely used with regard to God the Father. However, we will want to see if "God" is used as a stand-alone name for the second person of the Trinity in the New Testament, since if that is the case, it might also be true in the Old Testament.

A. Jesus is intimately associated with God

From the New Testament it is clear that Jesus is intimately associated with God. "Son of God" appears on 42 occasions, for example, and there are other similar terms such as "Holy One of God," "Messiah of God," and

---

[57] This is the first of many word counts reported in this chapter. As will be seen, these word counts will aid us in important ways in achieving the goals of our study. All word counts are based upon John R. Kohlenberger III, *The NIV Exhaustive Concordance of the Bible*, 3rd ed. (Grand Rapids: Zondervan, 2015).

"image of God." The power of God is in Christ, the wisdom of God is in Christ, Christ was sent by God, he was blessed by God, he followed God's will, he was the creator of the world with God, he is the very image of the Father, etc. The sum of all of this is that Jesus and the Father are one (John 10:31). Nothing here is new to Christians familiar with the New Testament.

B. Jesus is distinguished from God

In hundreds of cases in the New Testament, Jesus is distinguished from God. They are not the same person, and while they are often mentioned together, they are mentioned side by side as distinguishable beings. For example, the Apostle Paul routinely addresses the churches in his epistles extending grace and peace from "God our Father and the Lord Jesus

---

Outline
Studies of the Enduring Names for God

1. Studies of "God" in the New Testament
  A. Jesus is intimately associated with God
  B. Jesus is distinguished from God
  C. "God" is almost never a stand-alone name for Jesus

2. Studies of "Lord" in the New Testament
  A. Classification
    i. Immediate context
    ii. Other scriptures
    iii. Outside opinion
  B. God the Father
  C. Jesus the Son
  D. Holy Spirit
  E. Unclassifiable
  F. Conclusions

3. Multiple names for God in the New Testament

Christ" and on it goes. One is reminded of the medieval *Shield of the Trinity* referred to in chapter 1 (page 3) which shows that while all the members of the Trinity are God, each is distinguishable from the others. The only thing that will be new for many Christians in our study is the deliberate and detailed effort to distinguish between the first and second persons of the Trinity in the New Testament. That effort will assist greatly in finding Jesus at work in the Old Testament.

C. "God" is almost never a stand-alone name for Jesus

While the characteristics of God the Father are abundantly ascribed to Christ in the New Testament, "God" is almost never given to Christ as a single, stand-alone name. In fact, of the hundreds of times in which "God" is used as a single name in the New Testament, there is only one clear cut exception to this, where God the Father, in speaking of the Son, says, "Your throne, O God, will last forever and ever" (Hebrews 1:8). However, there are also three other cases in which Christ is referred to as God in almost but not quite stand-alone situations (John 20:28; Titus 2:13, 3:4). Even if one considers all four of these cases to be instances in which Jesus is called "God," 99.7% of the 1,440 uses of "God" in the New Testament refer to God the Father. It is therefore justified to establish a working rule that "God" used alone refers to the first person of the Trinity. Of course, "God" can be used in conjunction with other names to identify Jesus, and this is done on multiple occasions. Examples are "Son of God" (Matthew 14:33), "Holy One of God" (Mark 1:24), "Christ of God" (Luke 9:20), and "Lamb of God" (John 1:34).

While not the focus of our study, we can extend the basic finding just discussed about Jesus to the Holy Spirit. This can be done without much additional study because the results are the same. In fact, the Holy Spirit is never referred to in the New Testament simply as "God." Certainly, both Jesus and the Holy Spirit are God but, as a rule, neither are simply called "God."

In conclusion, as a single stand-alone name, "God" in the New Testament means God the Father in nearly every case. This finding will be helpful to us when we turn to the Old Testament and encounter "God" on numerous occasions.

2. Studies of "Lord" in the New Testament

We now turn to our study of "Lord" in the New Testament, and we quickly see that this study is considerably more complicated than our study of "God." First, just as we did for "God," we must put aside all appearances of "lord" where the reference is merely to another human being (such as one in a leadership or ownership position) rather than to the divine. As a proper name referring to the divine, "Lord" appears 616 times in the New Testament and "Lord's" appears 34 times (total of 650 occurrences). This is a little less than half as many occurrences as we saw with "God" (and "God's") in the New Testament (1,440). However, before we draw conclusions about the differences between these two numbers, we need to be aware that the numbers go in the other direction in the Old Testament ("Lord"/"Lord's," 7,010 times; "God"/"God's," 2,704 times). While one can puzzle at length on the differences here, it might be most productive simply to note that "Lord" and "God" are the most common words in the entire Bible when one has put aside nonspecific words such as "and," "the," "of," "for," and "a." Indeed, "Lord" with 7,660 appearances is by far the most common word in the entire Bible, and because of this, if we hope to understand the Bible, we need to grasp the full significance of this word.[58]

A. Classification

As "Lord" could refer to any member of the Trinity, each of the 650 uses of "Lord"/"Lords" in the New Testament was individually evaluated to see if there was evidence that it very likely or definitely referred to God the Father, very likely or definitely referred to God the Son, or very likely or definitely referred to the Holy Spirit. It was found that there were 110 cases in which it appeared that "Lord" very likely or definitely referred to God the Father, 515 cases in which "Lord" referred to Jesus, and zero in which the term was definitely applied as a name for the Holy Spirit. In the other 25 cases, there was not conclusive evidence pointing to a single and particular member of the Trinity. The classifications were made by taking the following steps:

i. The immediate context in which the word "Lord" appeared was examined, and in the majority of cases, this led to a straightforward classification. For example, no discussion is needed when one sees, "Lord Jesus Christ" or when someone comes up to Jesus and calls him "Lord." When the classification was not as obvious, the surrounding verses were examined, and they frequently rendered definitive information about who was being referenced. For example, if "Lord" was used a dozen times in a chapter definitively referring to Jesus, and the word "Lord" appears yet one more

---

[58] As previously noted, all word counts of the proper names of the divine are made with strict adherence to the NIV (2011) as reported by Kohlenberger III, *The NIV Exhaustive Concordance of the Bible (2015)*. The single exception was that "Lord's people" put in the place of "saints" in the New Testament text on 21 occasions was excluded from all the "Lord"/"Lord's" counts, the reason being that *kurios* was never found in the Greek on those occasions.

time in the chapter, it is not difficult to come to a conclusion as to whom "Lord" refers (e.g., 1 Corinthians 7).

ii. Other scriptures of direct relevance were examined. For example, frequently there are parallel passages in the gospels, and if the person referred to as "Lord" is not obvious in one of these passages, the parallel passages frequently render valuable information. Further, in a substantial number of cases, "Lord" appears in the context of a quote from the Old Testament, and in that event, a study of the passage quoted was done in order to come to a conclusion. In some cases, cross references were also helpful.

iii. Outside opinion was obtained. The 650 references were supplied to five reviewers for their comments, and every comment was carefully considered. When there was any significant disagreement as to classification of a reference with "Lord" in it, that reference was considered to be unclassifiable.

A listing of all 650 uses of "Lord" in the New Testament is found in the Appendix (page 129). The listing is according to the member of the Trinity referred to in each case. By referring to the Appendix, you can see how every appearance of "Lord" in the New Testament is classified. Let us now consider each of these three groups.

B. First Person of the Trinity: God the Father

There are 110 cases (17% of all uses of "Lord" in the New Testament) in which "Lord" very likely or definitely refers to God the Father. As examples, in Matthew 11:25 Jesus explicitly calls the Father "Lord of heaven and earth." In Luke 1:32, the angel tells Mary about her son who is to come, and the angel says that "the Lord God will give him the throne of his father David." "Lord" here must refer to God the Father. In Romans 11:3, Elijah is quoted as appealing directly to God and as calling him "Lord." While other examples could be cited, one particular quote from the Old Testament appears repeatedly in the New Testament and it requires care in interpretation.

The quote in question is from Psalm 110:1. This Psalm was written by David, and a portion of it says, "The Lord says to my lord…" Jesus' quote of this passage is found in Matthew 22:41–46, Mark 12:35–37, and Luke

20:41–44, and it is also cited by Peter in Acts 2:34. Jesus asked the Jewish leaders how the Christ could be the son of David and at the same time David could call him "Lord." It is clear from the gospel passages that the Jewish leaders of the time could not explain this—Jesus had them stumped, and Jews still struggle with it today.

> **Psalm 110:1**
>
> The Lord says to my lord: "Sit at my right hand until I make your enemies a footstool for your feet."

I consulted with knowledgeable Jews with regard to the meaning of Psalm 110:1. They pointed out that the two words for "Lord" are not the same in Hebrew, and they suggested that the second word pointed to an earthly leader such as a king who was in a special position. Such an interpretation is difficult to reconcile with the rest of the Psalm, such as verse 4 where it says that this person is "a priest forever in the order of Melchizedek." There is also the fact that the LXX renders both words the same (*kurios*), a rendering which cannot be put aside since the LXX is based on earlier Hebrew manuscripts than the Masoretic texts available today. In the end, the same conclusions were drawn which were implied by Jesus, namely, that the first "Lord" refers to God the Father and second to Jesus himself.[59]

C. Second Person of the Trinity: Jesus the Son

In 515 cases (79% of all uses of "Lord" in the New Testament), it was evident that Jesus was the member of the Trinity referred to by "Lord," and in the majority of these it was very clear. "Lord Jesus Christ" and similar wordings were commonly found which presented definite evidence that Jesus was the person referred to when "Lord" was used. In addition, there

---

[59] Persons wishing to dig further into this matter are invited to refer to Psalm 110:1 in their English translations and to see if the second "Lord" is capitalized or not. If it is, the translators are following the LXX but if it is not, the translators are following the Hebrew. However, scholars have found the Hebrew of this Psalm to be difficult to understand for a number of reasons. Jesus has the final word here by clearly indicating that "Lord" pointed to the divine in both cases. Thus, both should be capitalized. An agreement with this conclusion is found in essentially all English translations as they routinely capitalize both appearances of "Lord" in all New Testament quotes of Psalm 110:1, *even if they did not do so in the psalm itself.* Thus, Jesus and English translators of the New Testament side with the LXX over the Hebrew Masoretic text.

were several findings of special interest which emerged from the study of these 515 scriptures:

First, six Old Testament passages (Psalm 16:8, 110:1, 118:26; Isaiah 40:3, 53:1; Jeremiah 9:23–24) were cited in the New Testament in direct reference to Jesus, and each of these Old Testament passages referred to him as "Lord." Most of these passages were cited more than once in the New Testament, and altogether there were 15 such citations (Matthew 22:43, 44, & 45; Mark 1:3, 11:9, 12:36 & 37; Luke 20:42 & 44; John 12:38; Acts 2:25 & 34; Romans 10:16; 1 Corinthians 1:31; 2 Corinthians 10:17). It is reasonable to conclude that Jesus was called "Lord" in the Old Testament even though at that time the writers may not have appreciated the full significance of what they were writing under the guidance of the Holy Spirit.

Second, when people addressed Jesus face-to-face throughout the gospels, rarely did they call him "Jesus." In the gospels, he was addressed face to face 97 times with a name or title as follows (the first name or title is used when more than one is given): "Lord" 45 times, "Teacher" or "Rabbi" 35 times, "Jesus" seven times, "Master" five times, "Son of God" three times, "Son of David" two times, and "Son" once (Luke 2:48). Of further interest, on all seven occasions where he was called "Jesus," this was done by people who were not believers (demon influenced men, blind men, and lepers). On the other hand, both believers and nonbelievers addressed him as "Lord" including some people who were meeting him for the first time (Matthew 8:2, 9:28; Mark 7:28; Luke 7:6, 9:59, 18:41).

Third, an especially notable scripture is 1 Corinthians 8:6 which says, "...for us there is but one God, the Father, from whom all things came and for whom we live; and there is but one Lord, Jesus Christ, through whom all things came and through whom we live." "God" and "Lord" are thus clearly distinguished from one another, and there is but one of each.

D. Third Person of the Trinity: God the Holy Spirit

As God, the Holy Spirit is certainly entitled to be addressed as "Lord," but no *per se* case of this was found in the New Testament. This is true despite the fact that the presence of the Spirit was clearly manifested in the work of Jesus, and there are two especially relevant scriptures (Luke 4:18–19; 2 Corinthians 3:17–18). In the Luke reference which is a quote from Isaiah 61, Jesus clearly indicated that "the Spirit of the Lord" was on him. In 2 Corinthians, it says, "Now the Lord is the Spirit, and where the Spirit of the Lord is, there is freedom. And we all, who with unveiled faces contemplate the Lord's glory, are being transformed into his image with ever-increasing glory, which comes from the Lord, who is the Spirit." These are perhaps the clearest passages associating the Holy Spirit with divine Lordship. However, it appears to be the closeness of this relationship which is being established here, not the giving to the Holy Spirit the name "Lord." Overall, the conclusion is reached that the Holy Spirit is not simply called "Lord" anywhere in the New Testament.

E. Unclassifiable references to members of the Trinity

In 25 cases (4% of all uses of "Lord" in the New Testament), it was not possible to confidently attribute "Lord" to a single member of the Trinity. You are very welcome to study some of these 25 cases listed on page 132 and to see what conclusions you would draw. In addition, attention is drawn to the fact that it might be a mistake to assume that when "Lord" is used, it must always be in reference to a single member of the Trinity. Perhaps more than one member of the Trinity is being referred to in certain cases. This remains a theoretical possibility although it did not prove possible to identify uses of "Lord" in which two particular members of the Trinity were very likely involved (but not the third), or where it was certain that all three were involved.

F. Conclusions for our study of "Lord" in the New Testament

This study shows that the name "Lord" in the New Testament can refer to either God the Father or to God the Son, and in approximately 95% of the cases, "Lord" can confidently be identified as referring to one or the other. About 80% of the time it refers to the second person of the Trinity, and this overall finding is quite in contrast to the study of "God," where the single name "God" referred to God the Son at most 0.3% of the time. *It has become clear*

> **Summary—"Lord"**
>
> In round terms, in the New Testament "Lord" refers to:
>
> God the Father..........15% of cases
> Jesus..........................80% of cases
> Holy Spirit.................0% of cases
> Unclassifiable............5% of cases

that the words "God" and "Lord" do <u>not</u> typically have the same meanings. Therefore, there is value in distinguishing between them rather than using them interchangeably, even in the New Testament.

3. Multiple names for God in the New Testament

While we have focused on the single names of "God" and "Lord" in the New Testament, two or three names are sometimes put together. Of particular interest are names and titles added to the word "Lord" and that is what we will focus on here. All 650 occurrences of "Lord" as presented in the Appendix were again reviewed to determine the nature and frequencies of additional names and titles added to "Lord." Several results of interest emerged from this study:

A. Multiple names pointing primarily to God the Father

One group of compound names includes "Lord God," "Lord your God," "Lord our God," "Lord their God," "Lord God Almighty," and "My Lord and my God." The hallmark of this group of compound names is that in every case, the word "God" is included. In the entire New Testament, 30 of these were found, 28 of which were noted in passages which had been classified as referring to the first person of the Trinity (first section of the Appendix—page 129). The remaining two cases had been classified as referring to the second person of the Trinity, and they were "My Lord and my God!" (John 20:28, said by Thomas) and "Lord God" (Revelation 1:8).

B. Multiple names found pointing primarily to God the Son

A second group of compound names was found with the hallmark that "Lord" was always included but that "God" was not. The multiple names here included "Lord Jesus," "Lord Christ," "Lord and Christ," "Lord Jesus Christ," "Christ the Lord," "Jesus Christ our Lord," "Christ as Lord," and "Son Jesus Christ our Lord." In the entire New Testament, 137 of these were found, and, perhaps not surprisingly, every single one of these had been placed in the section of the Appendix pertaining to the second person of the Trinity. As would be expected, "Jesus" and "Christ" were especially common words added to "Lord," and when these additional words were used, the association of "Lord" with the second person of the Trinity was clear.

C. Multiple names found in unclassifiable references to members of the Trinity

In the 25 cases in which a particular member of the Trinity could not be identified as referenced when "Lord" was used, not a single one had any additional name attached to "Lord." This is in marked contrast to the two previous situations in which compound names had been found in about one quarter of the cases. In retrospect, it was evident that having even one additional name/title attached to "Lord" was very helpful in determining whether "Lord" referred to the first or the second person of the Trinity.

D. Conclusions regarding multiple names in connection with "Lord"

Overall, compound names including additions to the word "Lord" were found in 167 cases in the New Testament, and in every case a confident classification of "Lord" with a particular member of the Trinity had been made. As already indicated, the additional information provided by one or more names added to "Lord" was of substantial help in making a confident association of "Lord" with a particular member of the Trinity.

We have now completed the study of **Key #1—Enduring names for God**. As you can see, "God" and "Lord" are <u>not</u> equivalent terms, even in the New Testament. While most Christians use the terms interchangeably, in fact they have very different implications in terms of the persons in the Trinity to whom they refer. A summary of the findings for **Key #1** is presented in the top section of table 4. In the New Testament, "God" routinely refers to the first person of the Trinity, while in about four cases out of five "Lord" refers to the second person of the Trinity. When the names are used together, the first person of the Trinity is most commonly indicated but not always. All of these observations will be helpful in distinguishing between the first and second members of the Trinity when we turn to the Old Testament. First, however, we need to explore two other keys which will also assist us.

Table 4. New Testament studies: Summary from the application of the keys to distinguish the work of God the Father and God the Son		
Key	Findings pertaining to God the Father	Findings pertaining to God the Son
Key #1: **Enduring names for God**	"God" as a single name refers almost exclusively to God the Father. Further, multiple names for the divine which include "God" routinely implicated the first person of the Trinity.	"Lord" refers specifically to God the Son about 80% of the time and to God the Father in about 15% of the cases. About 5% of the time, the word "Lord" standing alone could not be confidently classified. Multiple names including "Lord" but not "God" routinely pointed to God the Son.
Key #2: **Primary roles of the divine**	Founder and administrator. Provided a foundation and set the stage for the New Testament. In the New Testament, he actively carried out his plan for the redemption of people and for drawing them to himself. Made no known physical appearances while undertaking his work.	Mediator between God and people. Prominent connection with people in speech and actions. Gave his life to make people acceptable to God. Conveys to people God's truth, God's will, and what needs to be known about God. His eternal nature includes his love for people to whom he provides comfort and direction.
Key #3: **Speech patterns of the divine**	At least as recorded in the New Testament, oral communications are infrequent, concise, given on important occasions, and focused on God the Son. They are not conversational in nature and do not include questions.	Oral communications are people-oriented, frequent, extended, and occur on a variety of occasions. They are often conversational in nature and they frequently include questions.

The interchangeable use of "God" and "Lord" by Christians is so universal that it is worth taking a moment to address whether such a use is "wrong." No, such a use is not incorrect simply because God the Father is definitely Lord and Jesus is definitely God. Further, in many cases it may not matter which person of the Trinity is being referred to, and in those cases the terms can certainly be used interchangeably. What our study has shown, however, is that some of the more subtle implications of the two names may be lost if they are used without attention to the differences between them, and especially so in regard to which member of the Trinity is being referenced. This, of course, is the focus of our study, and in this case distinguishing between these names has proven to be especially useful.

Key #2—Primary Roles of the Divine

Most Christians would agree that God the Father and God the Son have different roles—they do different things. If so, a study of these differences in the New Testament may help us to distinguish between these members of the Trinity. Therefore, we will now launch into a study of the primary roles of the first and second persons of the Trinity in the New Testament. We will then be able to take what we have learned to the Old Testament so that we can better understand the presence and work of these two persons there.

> **Key #2—Primary Roles of the Divine**
> **1. Primary Roles of God the Father**
>   A. Provided the plan and set the foundation for the New Testament
>   B. Actively involved in carrying out his plan
>
> **2. Primary Role of God the Son**
>   Mediator between God and people

1. Primary Roles of God the Father

Have you considered what roles God the Father plays in the New Testament? The reality is that we are so focused on Jesus, the Apostles, the church, and the teachings in the epistles that we often do not consider what God the Father may be doing. However, "God" is mentioned 1,440 times in the New Testament, and with such a large number, we must take some time to understand God the Father's roles there. From a review of "God" in the New Testament, there are two conclusions that seem especially obvious:

A. God provided the plan and set the foundation for the entire New Testament

God's work here is in addition to and beyond his role as creator and designer of the universe and all that is in it. If you simply read through the New Testament and take note every time "God" appears, it will be clear to you that God the Father provides the basis for all teachings and actions in the New Testament. He sets the standards, provides the commandments, and spells out the ways to meet those requirements with everything according to his plan. Several hundred references to God in the New Testament provide support for these comments. God's power and wisdom are evident, his actions constantly demonstrate that glory is due his name, and it is declared that God alone is good (Luke 18:19). When one turns to the question of sin, it is clear that sin must be dealt with, that only God can forgive sin, and that it was God who set up the plan for Jesus to come to pay the price for our sin so that we can be reunited with God.

B. God the Father is actively involved in carrying out his plan in the New Testament

If you read the New Testament with this assertion in mind, it is amazing to see how active God the Father is throughout these scriptures. He is involved from the very start in the execution of the plan for redemption which he established. Further, he sees the plan through step by step, and in so doing he clearly shows his profound love for us. Especially notable is the fact that he is identified as an agent of action, and specific actions of him are found 28 times in the first two chapters of Matthew and Luke. Reading these chapters, you see how God the Father delivers greetings and information by sending angels and through dreams. These divine messages reveal information concerning what is to come to pass and they provide instructions about what should be done. These communications make known God's master plan, and for both John the Baptist and Jesus, they provide the announcement, conception, birth, and naming. Everything was carefully done in preparation for the coming of our Savior.

Without a doubt, it was God the Father who sent the angel Gabriel to physically appear to Zechariah, promising a son despite his old age and that of his wife's, saying that the son was to be named John. He spelled out rules for his upbringing, and he declared what John would do for Israel (Luke 1:5–25). God did the same for Mary, again sending the angel Gabriel and giving her much information including the name she was to give her son (Luke 1:26–38). There were multiple appearances of an angel of the Lord to Joseph in four dreams giving him instructions to take Mary as his wife, to flee to Egypt, to return to Israel, and finally not to settle near Jerusalem but rather in Galilee (Matthew 1:18–25, 2:13–23). Explanations for all actions were given as the matters progressed. Stunning affirmations of God's actions were revealed through the Holy Spirit, who appeared to be involved at every point including in the affirmations and songs of Elizabeth, Mary, Zechariah, and Simeon (Luke 1–2). Overall, it is clear that God the Father had his hand in many different but carefully planned out actions to get our Savior here and in a position to do what the Father ordained.

Once Jesus was ready to begin his ministry, many citations can be made of the active involvement of the Father, especially in important events. The baptism of Jesus is one of these. We do not think about the Father having a hand in the selection of the disciples of Jesus, but before Jesus selected the full complement of disciples, he spent the night in prayer to God. Only then did he call the disciples and choose the 12 whom he named Apostles (Luke 6:12–16), so it seems reasonable to assume that the Father had a hand in this selection process. The Transfiguration also reveals the Father's hand. Much more can be said about the Father's presence during the ministry of Christ. God was there all along, right up to the end, even raising Jesus from the dead (Acts 4:10).

In summary, God's primary roles in the New Testament are as a founder, a plan setter, and an administrator in carrying out his plan. As we will see, these roles are remarkably different than those of God the Son.

2. Primary Role of God the Son

From a study of Jesus in the New Testament, it is clear that the roles of Jesus are much different than those of God the Father. His primary role is as mediator between God and people. 1 Timothy 2:5–6 spells this out very clearly: "For there is one God and one mediator between God and mankind, the man Christ Jesus, who gave himself as a ransom for all people." Further, it is clear that the revelation of God the Father is through God the Son: "No one has ever seen God, but the one and only Son, who is himself God and is in closest relationship with the Father, has made him known." (John 1:18). Other supporting scriptures include 1 Corinthians 8:6 and 2 Corinthians 3:18. Further, and as we will see in the section on speech patterns of the first and second persons of the Trinity, the second person of the Trinity does a great deal more talking to people than does the first. Thus, the Son of God is the usual way in which the divine communicates with humanity.[60]

Jesus is hugely people-oriented. Open a gospel of your choice to any passage where Jesus is active, and you will find that he is at work with people. He connects with people by coming to where they are and working with them there. In his connections, he is teaching, healing, and providing all kinds of assistance. Through it all he shows his love and that of God the Father for people. He is not focused upon starting schools, charitable organizations, or benevolent causes, even though these could help people tremendously. Nor is he focused upon political objectives such as liberating Israel from Rome. Instead, his focus is on people.

As the mediator between God and people, a huge objective of Jesus is to teach us about God. This includes instructing us about God's nature such as the will of God, the truth of God, the unsearchable love of God, and how to establish and maintain right relationships with God. This information provides a basis for the other teachings of Jesus including how to relate to people, which actions and thoughts are appropriate and which

---

[60] See Murray, *Jesus on Every Page*, 75-77, for an informative development of this position.

are not, and in general how to live. In addition, he prepares people for the life hereafter. And, he paves the way for forgiveness of sin by his own death on the cross so that all who believe in him may receive eternal life (Romans 6:23). In addition, he certainly provides comfort and direction.

The incredibly strong love of Jesus for people is a point which should not escape us. "As the Father has loved me, so have I loved you" (John 15:9). Such love is absolute, unshakable, and eternal, and this is the type of love that Jesus has for us as people. Furthermore, as the Romans passage indicates, nothing can separate us from this love. This love is in Christ Jesus—it is his very nature. Paul prays that we might be able "…to grasp how wide and long and high and deep is the love of Christ" (Ephesians 3:18). The Apostle John focusses upon the same point by saying, "This is how we know what love is: Jesus Christ laid down his life for us" (1 John 3:16).

> **Romans 8: 38–39**
>
> I am convinced that neither death nor life, neither angels nor demons, neither the present nor the future, nor any powers, neither height nor depth, nor anything else in all creation, will be able to separate us from the love of God that is in Christ Jesus our Lord.

PAUSE

In the recent COVID pandemic, thousands upon thousands of people found themselves separated from their loved ones, some of whom were in desperate medical condition, in hospitals, and even dying. The premier desire of these people was to be with their loved ones, regardless of the cost, but this desire was denied because of the pandemic. I can assure you that this was the case because my wife, Halie, was in the hospital and underwent a huge surgery to get rid of infection that could have taken her life. I wished nothing more than to be with her, but, I did not have the power to make this happen.

Now, what about Jesus? His love for people is incomprehensibly deep, it is unshakable, it is eternal, and it is part of his very nature. Further, since "Jesus Christ is the same yesterday and today and forever" (Hebrews 13:8), we are led to the conclusion that from the time that people were created, Jesus loved them and that this love continues to the present time.

If he loves people so dearly, would he not want to have been with them frequently throughout these thousands of years and especially so for those he has chosen and who are obedient to him? How could he want anything else, and if he wanted it, what could have prevented it from happening?

In summary for this section, the primary role of the Son of God is as mediator between God the Father and people whom he loves eternally. We have proven this in the New Testament, and where we find people chosen by God in the Old Testament, we may find Jesus there as well. If we do, we would expect to see him once again at work with those people. And, if we find him in this fundamental role, this will ring true with us because we know that his eternal nature is unchanging.

We have now completed the study of **Key #2—Primary roles of the divine**. A summary of our findings is found in the middle portion of table 4 (page 65). Even though our study has not been exhaustive, we have seen that the primary roles of the first and second members of the Trinity are markedly different. It is this difference which gives us hope that this key will be of assistance in distinguishing between the first and second persons of the Trinity when we turn to the Old Testament.

Key #3—Speech Patterns of the Divine

We now turn to a third key, a key which would be most unusual for theologians to propose but which to a behavioral scientist stands out as potentially quite useful. Fully 50 years ago (1970), I successfully completed a doctoral dissertation in Clinical Psychology at Purdue University in which the speech patterns of college students were evaluated and related to personality inventories. Perhaps it was this sensitivity to differences in speech patterns in general which drew my attention to the fact that God the Father and God the Son seemed to speak in dissimilar ways in the

> **Key #3—Speech Patterns of the Divine**
> 1. God the Father
> 2. God the Son

New Testament. I discovered that it is possible to develop speech profiles for the first and second members of the Trinity, and it was obvious that those profiles were quite different. I then wondered if those speech patterns might also appear in the Old Testament, and if so whether they would help us to discern who was speaking there. This whole approach is rather novel, and it will need to prove itself before it can be considered to be of value.

We need to begin this study by going to the New Testament to see if there are actually differences in the recorded speech of God the Father and God the Son. By the way, one cannot do this for the Holy Spirit since there is no identified speech in the New Testament for this third member of the Trinity.

1. Speech Patterns of God the Father

We are limited in our studies here simply because there are only three places in the New Testament in which the speech of the first member of the Trinity is recorded. One wishes that there were more places where speech of the Father is found, and especially that there was speech recorded in a broader range of situations. Nevertheless, let us look at these three and see what we can learn.

The first recording of speech by God the Father is at the baptism of Christ where a voice came from heaven which said, "You are my Son, whom I love; with you I am well pleased" (Luke 3:22). The same incident is reported in Matthew 3:17 and Mark 1:11 with words which are essentially identical.

The second recorded speech of the Father occurs at the Transfiguration of Jesus which is recorded in Matthew 17, Mark 9, and Luke 9 in very similar accounts. A voice from a cloud said, "This is my Son, whom I love; with him I am well pleased. Listen to him!" (Matthew 17:5).

The third account of speech from the Father occurs while Jesus was teaching about his own death during Holy Week. Jesus had just said, "Father, glorify your name!" and a voice came from heaven and said, "I have glorified it, and will glorify it again" (John 12:28). One can only conclude that these must be the words of God the Father.

One needs to again point out that while the above three cases are the sum total of all the recorded speech of God the Father in the entire New Testament, the total amount is small. Further, there is not a broad range of situations in which the Father speaks, and one wonders whether he would have spoken differently in other situations. Nevertheless, let us do what analysis we can of the speech which is available and specifically look at several key variables:

1. <u>Frequency of oral communications</u>. We can confidently say that recorded oral communications from God the Father in the New Testament are rare. "God" is mentioned some 1,416 times, but speech is recorded only three times.

2. <u>Length of communications</u>. The communications we have are very brief, and in fact they average around a dozen words each.

3. <u>Occasions on which speech is recorded</u>. Since we only have three communications to study, our conclusions in this area must be tentative. However, the three occasions on which God the Father speaks were very important ones, including the baptism of Jesus, the establishment that Jesus was indeed the Son of God at the Transfiguration, and the impending death of Jesus. Thus, his communications were specifically with regard to his Son, and they did not deal with a variety of human conditions, with covenants, with laws and commandments, or with other issues which would have lent themselves to more extensive communications. The importance of this limitation in the scope of topics addressed will become evident later in our studies.

4. <u>To whom the speech is directed</u>. On the first occasion, it was directed to Jesus, but it was in the hearing of everyone present. On the second occasion, it was directed to everyone present, and on the third occasion, everyone apparently heard it, even though it is not clear that they understood it.

5. <u>Apparent purpose(s) of the communication</u>. On all three occasions the communications show a strong connection between the Father and the Son, and the communications clearly make this known. In the first two cases, the Father's endorsement of the Son was clear and in the third case, the Son's affirmation of the Father was pronounced.

6. <u>Conversational emphasis in communications</u>. There were no conversations evident in the three verbal communications. They were straightforward declarations.

7. <u>Presence or absence of commands</u>. There is one command in the second communication, and this is for those in attendance to listen to Jesus and to do what Jesus says. The command is straightforward and to the point. The other communications had no commands.

8. <u>Presence or absence of questions</u>. There are no questions or inquiries in these brief communications. Note should be made that there are some authors who claim that God the Father asks many questions, but they routinely are referring to passages in the Old Testament and they also assume that "Lord" and "God" are interchangeable terms. As we have shown, this assumption is not tenable, and the entire claim of the first person of the Trinity asking questions becomes dubious.[61] Indeed, nowhere does it appear to have a solid foundation.

We have now completed a brief analysis of the limited information which we have of the speech patterns of God the Father as recorded in the New Testament. We especially wish that we had a broader and more numerous range of communications to study, but we studied all that were available and we drew what appeared to be reasonable conclusions based upon those. Let us go on and do a similar analysis of speech patterns of God the Son.

2. Speech Patterns of God the Son

In contrast to God the Father, there is much speech recorded of Jesus in the New Testament, and a study of it renders the following findings:

---

[61] A good example of an effort to assemble questions said to be asked by God the Father is the book by Israel Wayne, *Questions God Asks* (Green Forest, AR: New Leaf Press, 2014). Of the 19 questions which he believes God the Father asks, in the text 15 are asked by "the Lord" and not by "God." The remaining four (Genesis 18:9; Genesis 32:27; Numbers 22:9; Numbers 23:19) have peculiarities to them so that it is by no means clear that it is God the Father who is asking the question, and it is not always clear that a divine person is asking the question at all. For example, and in regard to Numbers 22:9, see the commentary on Balaam on pages 99-101. In summary, it was not certain that any of the 19 questions were actually asked by God the Father.

1. <u>Frequency of communications</u>. The frequency of the oral communications of Jesus as recorded especially in the gospels is high.
2. <u>Length of communications</u>. While some communications of Jesus in the gospels are brief, most are much longer and some are even chapters long. One of his prayers occupies a full chapter (John 17) and the Sermon on the Mount three chapters (Matthew 5–7), although it may have included parts of more than one sermon. His tendency to tell stories to get across points lends itself to more lengthy communications. Further, he almost never simply said "Yes" or "No" in response to a question. Instead, he often responded indirectly and frequently with a story. In general, his communications are not concise; instead, they have a fully developed quality to them that meets the complexities and intricacies of the situations that he is addressing.
3. <u>Occasions on which speech is recorded</u>. Jesus responded to a broad range of human experiences that he encountered during his ministry. For example, he spoke about paying taxes to Caesar (Matthew 22:15–22), he reacted to squabbles among his disciples (Matthew 20:20–28), he responded to the situation with regard to little children (Matthew 21:14–16), and he dealt with many other topics. He spoke of important theological issues as well, and it is fair to say that he taught on a wide range of topics.
4. <u>To whom speech is directed</u>. Jesus occasionally spoke to crowds of people and even thousands at a time (Matthew 14:13–21). More frequently, however, his speech is directed to specific persons, either single individuals or small groups.
5. <u>Apparent purpose(s) of the communication</u>. Typically, the recorded words of Jesus were for teaching, often with a particular emphasis on telling people about the will of God and frequently showing them how to carry out that will. Often, stories (parables) were used to provide a nuanced, in-depth understanding of God's will and how to carry it out.
6. <u>Conversational emphasis in communications</u>. A strong conversational emphasis is found in the speech patterns of Jesus. Back and forth verbal interactions with people were frequent, and

he even had conversations with God the Father which sometimes were for considerable periods of time.

7. <u>Presence or absences of commands</u>. The communications of Jesus contain many straightforward commands. Rarely would anyone walk away from a conversation with Jesus and not know what they should do.

8. <u>Presence or absence of questions</u>. The gospels record 307 questions which Jesus asked,[62] making this one of his most prominent speech patterns. Further, his tendency to ask questions went clear back to childhood. At the age of 12, for example, he remained in the temple in Jerusalem when his parents headed for home and they had to come back and get him. When they complained about his behavior, he simply asked two questions of them: "Why were you searching for me?" and, "Didn't you know I had to be in my Father's house?" (Luke 2:49). What was he doing for the three days it took for his parents to find him? He was sitting in the temple, listening to the teachers and asking them questions (Luke 1:46). Some of his last recorded words in the gospels were also a question which he asked and which was addressed to Peter (John 21:23). Further, even after his ascension his tendency to ask questions continued to be evident, and he called down to Saul on the Damascus road and asked, "Saul, Saul, why do you persecute me?" (Acts 9:4). Overall, the tendency of Jesus to ask questions in the New Testament is truly striking—it is a major feature of his speech.

We have now completed the study of **Key #3—Speech patterns of the divine** and a summary of our findings is presented in the bottom portion of table 4 (page 65). We are concerned that the speech available to us from God the Father is very limited, but we are going to push ahead anyway to see whether this key will prove worthwhile or not. Based on the information we have, we have seen striking differences in speech patterns between the first and second members of the Trinity. In the next chapter, we will see if these differences hold in the Old Testament, and if they are

---

[62] Martin B. Copenhaver, *Jesus is the Question* (Nashville: Abingdon Press, 2014).

useful there in identifying the presence of the first and second persons of the Trinity there.

Development of Guidelines to Apply the Keys

The focus of this chapter has been to present and test the usefulness of three keys in identifying and distinguishing between the presence and actions of God the Father and God the Son in the New Testament. The summary table 4 (page 65) demonstrates that each key does clearly distinguish between the first two members of the Trinity in the New Testament. This gives us hope that these keys will help us in making the same distinction in the Old Testament. The New Testament is a good place to test and refine these keys as there is little doubt about whether it is God the Father or God the Son who is the divine person in each passage studied.

While the keys are useful in distinguishing between the first two members of the Trinity in the New Testament, our objective is to apply them to the Old Testament to see if they are useful there in making the same distinction. It became evident that guidelines were needed to carry this out, and it further became evident that guidelines based upon the first key would be especially useful. Therefore, three guidelines were set up, and they are discussed below and are summarized in table 5 (page 78).

Guideline #1 applies to the circumstance in which "God" is the primary name of the divine person in the passage, with or without additional names but never including "Lord." Based on the findings from **Key #1** reported earlier in this chapter, it is routinely possible to immediately draw the conclusion that it is God the Father who is the divine person in the passage. This holds true throughout the New Testament, the only definite exception to being Hebrews 1:8 as previously discussed (page 57). If you wish to apply **Key #2** and **Key #3** to find confirmatory information, you may do so even though it is not required for **Guideline #1** as a conclusion has already been reached. In our New Testament studies, information provided by **Key #2** and **Key #3** was never contrary to the conclusion that it was God the Father who was involved. These are the general rules for **Guideline #1**.

Table 5. Guidelines based on the New Testament which are used to determine whether it is the first or the second person of the Trinity in the passages	
Names(s) of the divine person given in passage	Steps to take in order to reach a conclusion as to whether the first or second person of the Trinity is involved
Guideline #1: "God" is used either alone or with one or more other names (e.g., "God the Father") but without the use of "Lord" as any part of the name.	Go directly to the **CONCLUSION that this is the first person of the Trinity, God the Father.** If you wish to confirm this conclusion, apply **Keys #2 & 3** and in the New Testament, one or the other or both of these routinely provided definitive contextual information pointing to the first person of the Trinity.
Guideline #2: "Lord" is used either alone or with one or more other names (e.g., "Lord Jesus") but without the use of "God" as any part of the name.	As shown in the New Testament, likely this is the second person of the Trinity. However, as "Lord" can also apply to the first person of the Trinity, it is essential that you apply **Keys #2 & 3**, and the **CONCLUSION** that you draw will rest on the results from those keys. The experience with the New Testament has shown that you do not need to have the support of both keys in order to draw a conclusion—one is sufficient. No instance was found in which **Keys #2 & 3** led to different conclusions. If information is missing in the Biblical text on both keys, you cannot draw a reliable conclusion, and in that event, the **CONCLUSION is uncertain**.
Guideline #3: "God" and "Lord" are used together in one way or another to comprise a compound name.	In most cases, the first person of the Trinity is indicated when "God" and "Lord" are used together. However, this is not always the case and in every instance it is therefore essential to apply **Keys #2 & 3** in order to determine which member of the Trinity is being referenced. In the New Testament, those two keys will regularly lead you to a definitive conclusion as to the member of the Trinity who is involved.

Guideline #2 applies to the circumstance in which "Lord" is used as the primary name, with or without additional names, but never including "God." While in about 80% of the cases in the New Testament "Lord" refers to Jesus, that likelihood is not great enough to automatically draw that conclusion if used alone. In order to draw a firm conclusion, you must look for contextual information and especially that which allows you to apply **Key #2** and **Key #3**. Based on the references cited in the Appendix (page 129), our studies show that the information from **Key#2** and **Key #3** consistently provides reliable indicators of whether the first or second person of the Trinity is involved. However, if the reference to "Lord" is so brief that you cannot determine what is the primary role of the divine person (**Key #2**), and if the divine person never speaks in the passage (**Key #3**), then you cannot determine which person of the Trinity is being referred to because you do not have enough contextual information. This was true about 5% of the time in our studies of "Lord" (last section of Appendix, page 132), and in each of those cases, the particular member of the Trinity could not be determined.

Guideline #3 applies to the situation in which "God" and "Lord" are used together within a single name. "God Lord" never appears in the Bible, so it is "Lord God" which is at question here, as well as "Lord your God," "Lord our God," etc. Our studies of multiple names show that in most cases it is the first person of the Trinity who is referred to in this case. However, that is not always true, and as "Lord" could be either the first or second person of the Trinity, you must apply **Key #2** and **Key #3** to determine which member of the Trinity is involved. In the New Testament, the results of **Key #2** and/or **Key #3** applied in this situation regularly led to the conclusion believed to be correct as to which person of the Trinity was involved.

Conclusions

In this chapter we developed and individually tested three keys with regard to their ability to identify whether it was the first or the second member of the Trinity who was involved throughout the New Testament. We then developed three guidelines which allowed us to apply the keys systematically to the task at hand. We reached the following conclusions:

- **Key #1—Enduring names for God.** Our studies showed that the single names of "God" and "Lord" are not truly interchangeable in the New Testament. "God" almost invariably refers to the first person of the Trinity while "Lord" refers to the second person of the Trinity about 80% of the time. When the two names were used together, in most cases the first person of the Trinity was implicated but not always.

- **Key #2—Primary roles of the divine.** The first and the second persons of the Trinity have distinctly different roles in the New Testament. They are spelled out in this chapter and confirmed throughout the scriptures. The role of the second person of the Trinity with regard to people is especially notable, and his eternal love for mankind would logically be related to connections with people across the ages.

- **Key #3—Speech patterns of the divine.** While the first person of the Trinity spoke only on three occasions in the entire New Testament, it appeared safe to conclude that there were a number of important differences in speech patterns between the first and second persons of the Trinity. These differences were explored by evaluating eight different aspects of speech for both God the Father and God the Son.

- **Details about all three Keys** are summarized in table 4 (page 65).

- **Three Guidelines** were developed which lay out the procedures by which the keys can be applied, and they are given in table 5 (page 78). These guidelines were effective in identifying the particular members of the Trinity who were at work in passages throughout the New Testament.

We are now ready to move on to the Old Testament and to apply the keys and guidelines to multiple passages there. We will do this in the next chapter in an effort to determine if the keys and guidelines can reliably assist us in distinguishing between the first two members of the Trinity in the Old Testament, just as they did in the New Testament.

Five

The Old Testament: Finding Where Jesus is Likely at Work

Let us now take what we have learned in prior chapters and, using this information, see if we can discern where it is likely that Jesus was actually at work in the Old Testament. We immediately encounter a fundamental problem, however, and that pertains to how we will select parts of the Old Testament for study—we cannot study it all. The Old Testament is more than three times as long as the New Testament and it has 929 chapters, 23,214 verses, approximately 622,700 words (exact number depends upon the translation). Further, "God"/"God's" appears on 2,704 occasions and "Lord"/"Lord's" appears in 7,010 cases. Two approaches were considered to get the task at hand down to a manageable level.

First, one could set up a study approach with some sort of sampling plan in order to get the amount of material down to a workable level. You could, for example, study the contents of every tenth chapter. Such a plan would certainly be arbitrary and open to criticism, but there are other problems with it. Clearly, we want to study passages where the divine is at work, but such a plan might well omit major passages where the divine is at work and at the same time include other passages not directed to our objectives. Further, passing references to "God" and "Lord" with very little contextual information are frequently not helpful as there is often no description of any actions of the divine. Based on the New Testament studies of "Lord," we know that contextual information such as that provided by **Keys #2 & 3** is commonly needed to determine which member of the Trinity is involved. Considering all factors, this sampling plan approach to selecting scriptures for study has major disadvantages and limitations.

The second approach is to go through the Old Testament and select passages with descriptions of events or stories in which there is general agreement that the divine is at work. That would be the sole criterion for inclusion, and there would not even be a requirement that particular names for God (e.g., "God" or "Lord") be included. This would open the door as broadly as possible to evaluate which members of the Trinity are involved, the intention being to avoid a bias towards any particular member of the Trinity. Furthermore, the whole notion that there are just two enduring single names for God ("God" and "Lord") would be opened up for testing to see whether that contention is really supported in the Old Testament. If our premises are correct, and if there is consistency across the Old and New Testaments, we ought to find that the names for God are similar in the Old Testament as they are in the New Testament. We should also find that our keys and guidelines are routinely applicable as we sort out which member of the Trinity is involved in story after story in the Old Testament. This second approach was definitely preferable to the first, and it was the one which was adopted for our studies.

Note that our approach results in more passages being selected from some sections of the Old Testament than from others. In the Torah, for example, there are many accounts of the actions of the divine beginning with the creation of the world. The history and writings/poetry sections have fewer accounts of divine actions, so they would be expected to appear less often in our studies. At least several accounts from the prophets would be expected. As will be seen, these expectations were born out.

Old Testament Studies

The actual selection of the particular passages for study was accomplished by going through the Old Testament and finding events and occasions in which it was clear that the divine was involved. Initially, the aim was to select about 15 passages, but as it was discovered that some could be covered rather briefly, ultimately 25 were selected to permit the broadest testing possible while keeping this chapter to a manageable size. While there are more than 25 passages that would qualify for inclusion, it was discovered that this number would allow study of the vast majority of well-known passages. Giving a preference to those passages made sense, both because the accounts have meaning to most readers already, and because these passages do not require space-consuming descriptions (e.g., everyone already knows the basic story of Daniel and the den of lions).

In terms of limitations produced by the passage selection process, it is noted that no effort was made to find every single qualifying passage in the Old Testament. However, only two passages were considered and omitted (Genesis 16—Hagar, omitted as it was similar to other passages involving the angel of the Lord; Genesis 32—Jacob, unclear that he wrestled with a divine person—see Hosea 12:4). Every effort was made to insure that a bias was not introduced by these omissions or others, but as a reader you are welcome to search for other qualifying passages to see if you believe that there is any kind of bias in the passages selected for study.

Table 6 lists the 25 passages selected for study along with key information about each passage, including the conclusion as to the involved Trinity member(s). You can quickly go to the discussion on any passages of particular interest by referring to its page number in the first column of the table. We will now comment on all 25 passages in the order in which they appear in the Bible. The overall conclusions are presented following the comments on the 25 passages.

1. First Account of Creation—Genesis 1:1–2:3

This is the account of the creation with which we are most familiar. Except for a reference to the "Spirit of God" in Genesis 1:2, the deity is invariably called "God" throughout the entire passage. The applicable portion of table 6 is **Guideline #1**, and the conclusion reached is that the divine person in this passage is the first person of the Trinity. If you wish to confirm this using the other keys, it is certain that the primary role (**Key #2**) of the divine in this passage is creator and founder, just as would be expected. Further, if you look at the speech patterns (**Key #3**) of the divine in this passage, you will see that these patterns rather precisely match those expected for God the Father based on the New Testament. He speaks on important occasions, he is concise, he uses declarative sentences, his speech is not conversational in nature, and he asks no questions. Thus, using the information gleaned from our New Testament studies, the conclusion for which member of the Trinity is primarily involved here is very easy to draw.

If you have any concerns about the material in the last paragraph, it will likely be because you know that Jesus was also involved in the creation (John 1:2–3; Colossians 1:16–17; Hebrews 1:2). To better understand the role of Jesus in creation, read on.

Table 6. Summary of Old Testament passages to which the Guidelines and the Keys were applied						
Passage number (page number)	Topic/*passage*	Applicable Guideline(s)	Name(s) for God in passage Key #1	Person(s) in Trinity implied by Key #2	Person(s) in Trinity implied by Key #3	Conclusion: person(s) in Trinity in passage
1 (83)	Creation, First Account *Genesis 1:1–2:3*	#1	God	First	First	First
2 (86)	Creation, Second Account *Genesis 2:4–25*	#3	Lord God	Second	Second	Second
3 (88)	The Fall *Genesis 3*	#3	Lord God	Second	Second	Second
4 (90)	Noah and the Ark *Genesis 6–8*	#1 & 2	God (or Lord God), & Lord[63]	First & Second	First & Second	First & Second
5 (92)	Landmark communication Covenant with Noah *Genesis 9:1–17*	#1	God	First	First, but with long narration	First
6 (93)	Landmark communication Covenant with Abraham *Genesis 17*	#1	God	First	First, but with long narration	First
7 (93)	Visit to Abraham *Genesis 18*	#2	Lord	Second	Second	Second
8 (94)	Preparation for the Covenant with Moses *Exodus 3:1–11*	#2	Angel of the Lord, God, & Lord	Second	Second	Second

Passage number (page number)	Topic/passage	Applicable Guideline(s)	Name(s) for God in passage Key #1	Person(s) in Trinity implied by Key #2	Person(s) in Trinity implied by Key #3	Conclusion: person(s) in Trinity in passage
9 (96)	Landmark communication Covenant with Moses *Exodus 3:12–22*	#1	God	First	First, but with long narration	First
10 (97)	Deliverance from Egypt *Ex. 6:13–12:42*	#2	Lord	Second	Second	Second
11 (98)	Landmark communication Giving of the Law *Exodus 20:1–21*	#1	God	First	First, but with long narration	First
12 (98)	Particular Laws *Exodus 20:22–40:38 Lev. 1–27, Num. 1–19*	#2	Lord	Second	Second	Second
13 (99)	Balaam *Numbers 22–24*	#2	God,[64] angel of the Lord, & Lord	Second	Second	Second
14 (101)	Taking Possession of the Promised Land *Joshua 1–12*	#2	Lord	Second	Second	Second
15 (105)	Gideon *Judges 6–7*	#2 & 1	Angel of the Lord, Lord, & God	Second & First	Second; no speech by first	Second & First
16 (106)	Samson's Parents *Judges 13*	#2	Angel of the Lord	Second	Second	Second
17 (107)	Call of Samuel *1 Samuel 3*	#2	Lord	Second	Second	Second
18 (108)	Testing of Job *Job 1:6–2:10*	#2	Lord	Uncertain	Second	Second
19 (108)	Questioning of Job *Job 38–41*	#2	Lord	Second	Second	Second

Passage number (page number)	Topic/passage	Applicable Guideline(s)	Name(s) for God in passage Key #1	Person(s) in Trinity implied by Key #2	Person(s) in Trinity implied by Key #3	Conclusion: person(s) in Trinity in passage
20 (109)	The Lord Our Shepherd *Psalm 23*	#2	Lord	Second	No speech recorded	Second
21 (110)	When "God" is "Lord" *Isaiah 53*	#2	Lord	First	No speech recorded	First
22 (111)	Call of Jeremiah *Jeremiah 1*	#2	Lord	Second	Second	Second
23 (111)	Four Men in Fiery Furnace *Daniel 3*	#2	Angel of the Lord-LXX	Second	No speech recorded	Second
24 (113)	Daniel in the Den of Lions *Daniel 6*	#1	God	First	No speech recorded	First
25 (113)	Call of Twelve Prophets *Hosea thru Malachi*	#2	Lord[65]	Second	Second	Second

2. Second Account of Creation—Genesis 2:4–25

This account of creation has an entirely different flavor than the first because it is highly focused on people—it is anthropocentric. Further, the name for the deity has changed from "God" to "Lord God." If you look through this passage, you will see that only "Lord God" is used as the name for the divinity and never "God." I believe that the Holy Bible was put together under the direction of the Almighty. The personal styles of writers show through and favorite words are used by certain writers. However, I believe that key terms such as the names for God were core parts of the revelation, that the writers received them and faithfully put them down. Thus, I do not believe that Moses (or whoever wrote Genesis) woke up one day and happened to use "Lord God" whereas the previous day he happened to use "God." Further, note that whereas "Lord God" appears several times in the Old and New Testaments, "God Lord" never

---

[63] See text for comments on the differences here between the Hebrew and the Greek (LXX).

[64] See the likely explanation in the text for the use of "God."

[65] See the likely explanation in the text for the use of "God" with regard to Jonah.

appears even once. Thus, a plan is evident—these names are not put in the Bible haphazardly.

A notable Jewish writer, Dennis Prager, gives us some insights into the reasons for the change from "God" to "Lord God."[66] He notes that "God" in Genesis 1 comes from the Hebrew *Elohim*. God is the creator and he needs only to will it, and it is done. He is the one who composes order out of chaos. He is the ultimate good that we cannot approach as he is transcendent. The introduction of "Lord" into this second account of creation brings in a "personal God" (*Yahweh, YHVH* or *YHWH*) who shows concern for the needs of human beings. This includes mercy in a prominent way, and this is in contrast with *Elohim* who has an emphasis on justice. These insights are helpful in making distinctions between "God" and the "Lord God."

One more thought will be offered here, and that is whether the use of "Lord God" could have been one of the steps that God took to reveal the Trinity. In Genesis 1:1, *Elohim* is the name for God but *Elohim* is plural. Interesting! Using the Hebrew interlinear,[67] "the Spirit of God" is referred to in verse 2. While the Jewish Tanakh translation uses the term "wind" in place of "spirit," the LXX points to the latter with *pneuma*. In Genesis 2:4, the word "Lord" is introduced and that name is paired with "God" 20 times in chapters 2 and 3. Beginning with Genesis 4:1, "Lord" stands alone, and in most cases "Lord" is used alone through the rest of the Old Testament. Neither Jews nor Christians doubt that "Lord" is divine, and this pairing of "Lord" and "God" seems to have set the stage for this understanding. However, perhaps it was also intended to introduce the second member of the Trinity who is the "personal God" referred to by Dennis Prager, a God with a focus upon people.

As the focus of the divine in the present passage is on the connection with the man, we have a specific interest in **Key #2**, namely, the role of the divine. The Lord God puts the man in the garden, he directs his work there, he gives instructions with regard to a particular tree (Genesis 2:16–17), he asks the man to name all the animals, and he notes what name

---

[66] Dennis Prager, *The Rational Bible: Genesis—God, Creation, and Destruction* (Washington, DC: Regnery Faith Publishing, 2019), 32.

[67] Jay P. Green, Sr., *The Interlinear Bible: Hebrew-Greek-English* (Peabody MA: Hendrickson Publishers, 1984).

the man give to "each living creature" (Genesis 2:19). The Lord God also provides a help-mate and companion for the man. Thus, while certainly a mediator between the man and the divine, the Lord God is concerned with the man, interested in his opinions, and attentive to his needs.

In terms of speech patterns (**Key #3**), conversations must have occurred between the Lord God and the man on matters such as caring for the garden and the naming of animals (Genesis 2:19–20). How else could instruction have been given to the man and how else could names for the animals been obtained other than by asking him questions about what he would name each animal? With no mention of visions or dreams, these contacts may have been in person.

In and of itself, the name "Lord God" is not definitive in pointing to a particular member of the Trinity according to **Guideline #3** (page 78), but both the second and third keys point to the second member of the Trinity, so that is the conclusion we will draw. If you are not sure, you will want to decide which other member of the Trinity it was and why.

3. The Fall—Genesis 3

This is the story of Adam and Eve eating the fruit of the tree of the knowledge of good and evil which they had been forbidden to do, and of what followed that sinful act. The Lord God comes on the scene in verse 8, and once again **Guideline #3** is applicable. That guideline requires us to get information on **Keys #2 & 3**. With regard to **Key #2**, it could hardly be clearer that the Lord God is serving as a connector between God and people. The Lord God must have appeared to Adam and Eve in bodily form or they would not have heard him walking in the garden as is clear in verse 8. The three of them must have stood there and talked face to face. The Lord God talked rather directly about their sin, both Adam and Eve gave their excuses, and the Lord God handed out the penalties.

Going to **Key #3**, the speech patterns of the Lord God were especially revealing. His speech started off with a question (Genesis 3:9), just as did the first recorded speech of Jesus in the New Testament (Luke 2:49). By the time one gets to verse 14 of Genesis 3, the Lord has asked four more questions—a total of five! At no place in the Bible does God the Father speak in this way. Furthermore, the communications here are clearly conversational in nature and face to face—something never found with God the Father in the New Testament. Clearly, the speech pattern of the Lord God in this passage is similar to that of the second person of the Trinity in the New Testament. Finally, there are the scriptures that declare that no one has seen God at any time (Exodus 33:20; John 1:8; 1 John 4:12), but they *never* say that no one has seen the Lord at any time.

If one accepts the keys and guidelines based on the New Testament, one can only conclude that it is the second person who is the Lord God in this passage.

PAUSE

Let us pause a moment here to think about what we have covered in only three Old Testament passages, and reflect on the conclusions which are being drawn. To be clear, I am proposing here that Jesus appeared to people in bodily form in the Garden of Eden. He walked with them and he talked with them so it was not necessary to wait for the incarnation for this to happen. If you are able to get your mind around this, you will see that your Savior has always cared about people clear back to their appearing on the earth, working with them through troubling times, sometimes face to face. If you do not think it was Jesus who did this, then which member of the Trinity do you think it was, and why?

We know from the gospels that the nature of Jesus is to deeply and truly care for people, and since "Jesus Christ is the same yesterday and today and forever" (Hebrews 13:8), we should entertain the possibility that he cared for people through the Old Testament as well. Would not that make a lot more sense than to assume that he must have sat in heaven for thousands of years, waiting for Bethlehem and meanwhile doing very little while his people were enslaved and endured many miserable circumstances on earth? And, would it not also make a lot more sense than to say he cares hugely for people but that he has spent only three years on earth ministering to them since the creation of the world? Considering such questions may help us to gain new understandings of the nature of our Savior.

There is one more matter here which should at least be raised. You may be vexed by what was said to Adam and Eve in Genesis 3:16–19. It is easy to think, "It's not fair," when, due to the sin of Eve and Adam, you read of all women for all time having to suffer pain in childbirth, and for men having to work throughout their lives, toiling with discomfort and sweat in order to make a living. What is worst is that if one says that the Lord God is the second person of the Trinity in these passages, then it is Jesus who is handing down these sentences. However, if you go back and look at the difficult teachings of Jesus in the New Testament which we previously covered (pages 8-11), you will see that these teachings are little different in severity than the teachings of Jesus in the New Testament. In both cases they do not conform to twenty-first century western standards of social justice. Therefore, they are both difficult for many to accept, but it is not really clear that those in the Old Testament are worse than those in the New Testament.

---

4. Noah and the Ark—Genesis 6–8

This is one of the best examples of the use of both "God" and "Lord" as separate names in the entire Old Testament, first one name and then the other. You will find this in your English translation which likely follows the Hebrew closely. In Genesis 6:5–8 the "Lord" recounts the evil on the earth and his desire to destroy that evil. In Genesis 6:11–22, it is "God" who gives detailed instructions on the building of the ark. In 7:1–5, the "Lord" gives instructions about going into the ark. In 8:1–19, "God" brings the flood to an end, and he instructs Noah about getting all living things out of the ark. Finally, in 8:20–22, Noah built an altar to the "Lord," and the "Lord" responds positively to the sweet-smelling sacrifice.

Overall, the sections present actions by "Lord," "God," "Lord," "God," and "Lord," and both **Guideline #1** and **Guideline #2** apply. However, there are some problems here. For one thing, at first reading it appears that "Lord" and "God" are used quite interchangeably, raising a question about the validity of **Key #1**. Further, the primary roles of "God" and "Lord" are anything but distinctive, and they raise a question about **Key #2**. Also, **Key #3** comes to our attention as the speech patterns do not conform to expectations for "God" and "Lord," especially because the detailed instructions on how the build the ark are in no way characteristic of the first person of the Trinity, at least as found in the New Testament.

Taken together, on first review, more things appear to be out of line with our keys than on any other passage we have looked at in either the Old Testament or the New Testament.

As it turns out, all of the concerns noted in the last paragraph are resolved by the LXX because the names for the divine depart from those in the Hebrew on many occasions in these three chapters. Genesis 6:6–7 is the first example of this and English translations which are based on the Hebrew say something like, "The Lord regretted that he had made human beings on the earth, and his heart was deeply troubled. So the Lord said, 'I will wipe from the face of the earth the human race I have created." Based on our New Testament studies, we know that the overall authority in the narration here, plus its brevity, are much more characteristic of the first person of the Trinity than the second. In fact, the LXX uses "God" and not "Lord" in both cases in these two verses and the difficulty is resolved.

A second example of resolution of problems by the LXX is found in Genesis 6:13 where English translations record a long series of instructions given by "God" on how to build the ark. However, from our studies we know that giving such detailed instructions is much more characteristic of the second person of the Trinity than the first. In this case, the LXX says "Lord God" rather than "God," and as we may interpret this as a reference to the second person of the Trinity such as is seen in Genesis chapters 2 and 3, this problem disappears.

In a third example of resolution by the LXX, particulars on how to get out of the ark are said to be from God in Genesis 8:15, but the LXX says "Lord God." In sum, if you use the same Old Testament that the early church used, the LXX, you will not detect any discrepancies at all, and the validity of all three keys is supported rather than being called into question.

You can see why an entire chapter in this book was spent on the LXX. The LXX promotes seeing similarities in the names, roles, and communication patterns of the first and second persons of the Trinity across the Old Testament and the New Testament. As such, it reinforces the contention that the roles and communication patterns of the first and second persons of the Trinity are similar across both testaments and yet clearly different from each other. As a result, the validity of using the same keys to distinguish between the first and second persons of the Trinity throughout the whole Bible is strengthened. In making these comments, I am not proposing that the Hebrew text be abandoned, but rather that a simultaneous consideration of both texts is both justified and likely to lead to the best understanding of Old Testament passages.

In conclusion for this section of scripture, both **Guidelines #1 & 2** apply, and both the first and second members of the Trinity are involved.

5. Covenant with Noah—Genesis 9:1–17

This is the first of four unusually important communications from God, and we will call them <u>landmark communications</u>. To understand the essential features of these, read the adjacent text box.

After all living things leave the ark, Noah builds an altar and offers a sacrifice to the Lord (Genesis 8:20–22). The Lord's response to this is very positive, and it includes a vow to never again destroy all living creatures.

God's communication with Noah

> **Landmark Communications**
>
> Three covenants and the giving of the law are four extremely important communications from God to people. Each has the following features:
>
> 1. Preparation for the event by the Lord alone.
> 2. Presentation of the content by God alone in a relatively long monologue.
> 3. Any and all follow-up by the Lord alone.

and his sons immediately follows (Genesis 9:1–17). The first part of this contains a blessing and some commands (verses 1–7), and then the very important covenant follows (verse 8–17). **Guideline #1** applies to this passage and it does not require the application of either **Key #2** or **Key #3** as it automatically results in the conclusion that it is the first person of the Trinity who is involved. Nevertheless, it is noted that **Key #2** reinforces that conclusion as does the nature of the narration (**Key #3**) except that the narration is relatively long for the first person of the Trinity. That fact likely reflects the importance of the occasion with the establishment of a covenant. As there is no situation like this in the New Testament in which God spoke, the longer narration was not anticipated. However, it was found here and it will be found in each of the three other landmark communications which we are covering.

6. Covenant with Abraham—Genesis 17

Our second <u>landmark communication</u> is the covenant with Abraham. It was the Lord who did the groundwork here by first getting Abram to leave his land and to go to Palestine (Genesis 12:1–5). There is an extended conversation between the Lord and Abram in Genesis 15. After the story of Hagar in chapter 16, the Lord again appears to Abram (Genesis 17:1–2) in preparation for the giving of the covenant. Immediately, the covenant is given by God beginning in verse 3 and **Guideline #1** is applicable. There is no problem if one wishes to apply **Key #2**, as this is God's role and not the Lord's.

With regard to **Key #3**, the covenant made with Abraham had another feature similar to the covenant with Noah, and this was that God's speech was also relatively long—some 20 verses. This was, of course, the pivotal covenant on which the whole Jewish nation was based. It included the promise of nations and lands, the renaming of Abram and Sarai, commands including circumcision, the promise of Isaac despite the ages of his parents, and the destiny of Ishmael. All of this is a lot to get into 20 verses, but God is concise and he did it. It was the Lord who followed up with Abraham in chapter 18 to which we will now turn.

7. Visit to Abraham—Genesis 18

No time was wasted before the Lord (not God) visited Abraham and Sarah with two angels. **Guideline #2** applies. The Lord had bodily form or he could not have eaten the food provided (verse 8). This occasion reminds us about how Jesus ate food when he suddenly appeared to the disciples after his visit to Emmaus (Luke 24:41–43). The divine person here clearly performed the role of a mediator (**Key #2**), both to convey God's will about the son who was to come and then in connection with Sodom and Gomorrah. Also, note the Lord's speech (**Key #3**) through the chapter which was extended and which was unusually conversational as the Lord and Abraham bargained at some length (vv. 23–33). The Lord also asked several questions (vv. 13–17), which we have established as a key feature of the speech of the second person of the Trinity. Indeed, it is very difficult to imagine any other divine person being "the Lord" in the passage at hand.

Being with people face-to-face, eating, and negotiating with humans are unheard of for the first and third members of the Trinity.

I asked my Jewish friends about the use of "Lord" in this passage and to whom the term refers. Many Jews believe that there are three angels and that one simply speaks on behalf of (or in the name of) the Lord. According to this viewpoint, none of the three are divine. However, this is quite difficult to reconcile with the facts that one of them was repeatedly called "Lord," that one of them had the ability to provide an heir, and that one had the ability to destroy a city. As it is reasonable to believe that such powers rest only with the divine, a second Jewish opinion expressed to me is that during the conversation, the Lord himself came down and became involved in the interchange.

8. Preparation for the Covenant with Moses—Exodus 3:1–11

While Moses was tending the flock of his father-in-law, "the angel of the Lord" appeared to him (Exodus 3:2). We need to know who "the angel of the Lord" is as the term appears more than 40 times in the Old Testament and as we will be studying three more passages that have the term in it. Detailed summaries of various theological perspectives on the term are available for interested persons,[68] but rather than going into those perspectives in detail, it would be worthwhile merely to note in summary form what is apparent from the many relevant passages.

As succinctly summarized in an unpublished document,[69] "the angel of the Lord" is deity for the following reasons: 1) he is spoken of as divine (Exodus 3:2–6,13–15); 2) he himself speaks as deity (Genesis 22:11–12, 15–16; 2 Kings 1:3–5); 3) those to whom he appears recognize him as divine and call him God (Genesis 16:13; Judges 6:22; Judges 13:21–22); 4) he is offered and accepts both worship and sacrifice (Judges 13:19; 1 Chronicles 1:18–19); 5) he has divine attributes, prerogatives, and authority performing miracles and signs (Genesis 48:15–16; Judges 2:1–2; Judges

---

[68] James A. Borland, *Christ in the Old Testament* (Ross-shire, Great Britain: Christian Focus Publications, 2010).

[69] Unpublished manuscript by Rev. Thomas Brewer of Bellevue, WA, USA entitled, "An angel we ought to know." Available upon request. Murray, *Jesus on Every Page,* 77-85 presents somewhat similar information.

13:3; 2 Kings 19:35; Psalm 35:4–6); 6) he speaks promises and prophecy and brings them to pass (Genesis 6:10; Zechariah 3:3–7); and, 7) he forgives sins in some cases and renders judgments in others (Genesis 22:15–18; Exodus 23:21; Numbers 22:32; Judges 2:1–3; Psalm 34:7). There is also evidence that the angel of the Lord can appear physically so that even an animal can see him (Numbers 22:21–33).

Presuming that the flock of scriptures just referenced has convinced you that "the angel of the Lord" is divine, why the term "angel" at all? The association must be because of his function as one who was sent, a messenger, a mediator, and not because of his nature which is divine. Further, it is of interest that the term applied to this person always starts with the definite article "the." Thus, it is not "an angel of the Lord" but "the angel of the Lord." The implication is that there is only one such angel. The last time that this phrase appears in scripture is in Matthew 1:24, after which, with the birth of Christ, the term never appears again in the Bible. Indeed, the messenger of the Lord had come, the Lord himself.

"The angel of the Lord" appeared to Moses in the flames of the burning bush (Exodus 3:2), and this is part of the passage describing the preparation for the giving of the covenant with Moses by God. As is true in the other landmark passages we are studying, it is contended that this preparatory work is done by "the Lord" and not by God. How can this be when the Hebrew text plainly uses "God" as the speaker not once but twice? It is only possible

> **Exodus 3:3–6. Key words in both (NIV) and [LXX]**
>
> So Moses thought, "I will go over and see this strange sight—why the bush does not burn up." When the Lord saw that he had gone over to look, **(God) [the Lord]** called to him from within the bush, "Moses! Moses!" And Moses said, "Here I am." "Do not come any closer," **(God) [he]** said. "Take off your sandals, for the place where you are standing is holy ground." Then he said, "I am the God of your father, the God of Abraham, the God of Isaac, and the God of Jacob." At this, Moses hid his face, **(because he was afraid to look at God) [for he venerated to look in the presence of God].**

because while your English translation in verse 4 very likely says something like "God called to him from within the bush," the LXX reports that it is the Lord who called, not God. Further, at the start of verse 5 and again according to the LXX, it is not "God said" but "he said," which would in the LXX refer to the Lord who is talking. Thus, a very different perspective is given with the change of exactly two words. A puzzlement is also cleared up as to why "God" would call to Moses just because the "Lord" saw that Moses went over to the bush. The passage now flows smoothly, and it ends in a more understandable way with the LXX saying that Moses was greatly in awe and respect in the presence of God rather than saying that he was afraid to look at God which would imply that God was standing there and could be seen.

There is still more to be found in this passage. First, "the angel of the Lord" in verse 2 is now simply "the Lord" in verse 4 and following. Exactly the same simplification is also found elsewhere with the implication that "the angel of the Lord" = "the Lord" (Judges 6:11–16). Further, the assertions of the speaker that he himself is the "God of your father, the God of Abraham, the God of Isaac and the God of Jacob" are entirely in order because indeed, the Lord is God. Also, there is a similarity between this passage and others where "the Lord" worked with and intervened for Abraham (Genesis 18), Isaac (Genesis 24), and Jacob (Genesis 28). Moses rightly shows a real reverence for the presence of the Almighty. What he did not know was that it was God the Son (the "Lord") in front of him, not God the Father. Of interest is the fact that this conclusion was exactly that of Justin Martyr more than 1,800 years ago.[70] Clearly, the second person of the Trinity was at work with final preparation for the covenant starting in verse 7.

9. Covenant with Moses—Exodus 3:12–22

This is the third landmark communication that we are studying. The importance of the occasion is huge as it was the call to Moses to deliver the nation of Israel out of Egypt. In the very first sentence, God assures Moses that he will be with him. While the covenant is surely made by God's saying, "I will be with you," Moses responds with a question about God's identity to which God responds with the famous "I Am" statement (Exodus 3:14). God tells Moses what is going to happen and he gives a

---

[70] Wilhite, *Is Jesus YHWH?*, 65.

number of details about the deliverance that will occur. The last line is that Israel "will plunder the Egyptians" (Exodus 3:22).

Clearly **Guideline #1** applies and nothing from the Lord is recorded during the giving of the covenant. If one were to apply **Keys #2 & 3**, we would have no trouble with **Key #2**, but as with other landmark communications, God speaks more than expected, again likely due to the gravity of the situation. Further, as was seen with Abraham in Genesis 17:18–22, there is a bit of dialogue with the person receiving the covenant recorded in Exodus 3:13-14. The importance of this communication with Moses is at the highest level with the deliverance of God's people at stake. There is nothing like this in the New Testament or perhaps we would have seen God respond in a similar way there.

When the giving of the covenant by God is completed at the end of the third chapter, it is the Lord who comes on to the scene as the fourth chapter starts. The stage is set for the appearances to Pharaoh with the establishment of two signs to impress the Egyptians (Moses' staff thrown down becomes a snake; Moses' hand in and out of his cloak becomes leprous). Aaron joins the team and the Jewish people get on board as well. The Lord manages everything in that chapter and he demonstrates his tendency to ask questions with four of them in a row in Exodus 4:11!

10. Deliverance from Egypt—Exodus 6:13-12:42

These chapters are filled with the events that led up to the nation of Israel finally being released from bondage in Egypt. The Lord directs this entire effort beginning with convincing Moses and Aaron to take on the task of leading the nation out. Then they have contacts with Pharaoh in connection with each one of the 10 plagues. The Lord gives numerous commands and directions in these seven chapters, and in fact "Lord" is mentioned 106 times while "God" is mentioned just 18 times. Further, in contrast to the hundreds of lines of speech from the "Lord," "God" does not contribute even one word. Students of the Bible should really be struck with this difference in this section of the scriptures as "God" and "Lord" are remarkably different in these several chapters.

Invoking **Guideline #2**, we need to look at the primary role (**Key #2**) and speech patterns (**Key #3**) of the Lord. Actually, each appearance of the Lord requires only a glance because it is obvious that the Lord is the mediator here and his speech is very similar to that of the second person of the Trinity in the New Testament.

11. Giving of the Law on Mt. Sinai—Exodus 20:1–21

This is the fourth and final <u>landmark communication</u> which we are studying, and like the other three, it is of huge importance. Also, just like the others, the Lord paves the way (Exodus 19:9–25). Acting as a mediator and communicating through Moses, the Lord tells the people what is about to happen, and he gives instructions about what they should do in preparation for it. The people are consecrated by Moses, they wash their clothes, they abstain from sexual relations, and they may not climb upon the mountain. Then, final instructions are given to Moses while on the top of the mountain, and these include going down to give the people warnings about not encroaching on the mountain itself. Finally, Moses is to come back up with Aaron. The stage is now set for the giving of the Law, and the Lord's preparatory work is done.

God alone speaks in Exodus 20:1–17 and he presents the fundamentals of the law in the form of the 10 commandments. **Guideline #1** clearly applies and absolute directives are handed down by God as he assumes his expected role (**Key #2**). While most of the commandments are concise, they do add up to 17 verses. Exactly as with the other three landmark communications, the importance of the event is truly monumental, and while the speech is longer than might be expected, its character is otherwise similar to that of the first person of the Trinity (**Key #3**). There is no evidence that the Lord is involved in this event in any way, but immediately thereafter he does launch into the follow-up.

12. Giving of Particular Laws—Exodus 20:22–40:38, Leviticus 1–27, Numbers 1–19

With God's giving of the 10 commandments and thereby underpinning the entire law, the Lord at once begins to spell out what all of this means (Exodus 20:22). Specific commandments about worship are given in verses 22–26, and adherence to these provides the foundation for the host of particular commandments that begin in chapter 21. Exodus 21:1 quotes the Lord saying to Moses, "These are the laws you are to set before them." The Lord then lays down the laws to Moses, and it takes 66 chapters to do so. The rest of Exodus is consumed with this activity as is the entire book of Leviticus and the first 19 chapters of Numbers. After all, only 10 commandments had been given thus far by God, and since the Jews have carefully counted all the commandments and have found 613, we have about 600 to go!

There are four kinds of information given in the 66 chapters in Exodus, Leviticus and Numbers: 1) laws; 2) instructions about building the tabernacle and its furnishings, and what the priests and others are to do in that setting; 3) assurances and reconfirmation of the covenant; and, 4) historical information about how the people of Israel responded during this period. Throughout all the chapters, it is the Lord who does the speaking and the commanding, and not God. The instructions are often incredibly detailed such as in Exodus 26 with regard to the construction of the tabernacle. **Guideline #2** applies to this very long section of the Old Testament, and **Keys #2 & 3** provide support to the second person of the Trinity being "the Lord" throughout this extended section of scripture.

13. Balaam—Numbers 22–24

We come to an unusual passage which requires close attention. The whole incident starts when Israel approaches the promised land and the king of Moab becomes worried that Israel will destroy his kingdom. The king sends a message to Balaam, a prophet, and offers to pay him a fee to come and curse the nation of Israel. When the messengers from the king come with the money, Balaam clearly considers the request and tells them to wait the night while he inquires of the Lord as to what to do. During the night, God comes to Balaam, asks him who the messengers are, and tells him not to go back with them. The next morning, Balaam declines the job, "...for the Lord has refused to let me go with you" (Numbers 22:13). The king sends another envoy with the same request and promises even more money, but instead of turning the job down as a true prophet would, Balaam again considers it, tells the messengers to stay the night and that he will again ask the Lord. We do not know exactly what happened, but possibly after extensive pleading with the divine during the night, he is given permission to go but only to say what he is told to say.

When Balaam mounts his donkey the next morning and heads out to do the cursing of Israel, God is very angry that he is going at all (Numbers 22:22). He should know better. The angel of the Lord stands in his way with a drawn sword and blocks him three times. Even the donkey can see the angel of the Lord, but in his spiritual blindness, Balaam cannot. Thus, he beats his donkey three times to get her back on the road, and an interesting conversation with the donkey ensues. Finally, Balaam's eyes are opened, he sees the angel of the Lord, he realizes that he has sinned, and he offers to go back (Numbers 22:34). The angel of the Lord tells him to go ahead with the men, but to speak only what he is told to speak. In fact, Balaam does that and he blesses the nation of Israel rather than cursing it.

The idea that a prophet of God would prophesy for money or personal gain is unknown in the Old Testament except for this one incident. The fact that his reputation went from where he apparently lived in Syria some 400 miles to Moab[71] may very well mean that his willingness to be bought off was widely known. That he would even consider cursing the nation of God is in and of itself truly reprehensible, and any covenant with God was clearly broken by Balaam. Earlier, we quoted a Jewish writer who indicated that the word "Lord" implies a personal God who is merciful and who has a concern for the welfare of human beings (page 87).[72] "Lord" is the term which is used constantly in connection with the true prophets and a covenant relationship is implied. This word was not used with Balaam through all the initial contacts with him, but rather "God." With the covenant broken, the writer uses "God" instead of "Lord" and this implies a more distant relationship and one which accentuates the difference between the holy and pure deity and the errant prophet.[73] The informed reader would be struck by this difference in terms, and if one accepts this explanation for the use of "God" instead of "Lord," the contention that "God" asks a question in Numbers 22:9 disappears.

Additional support for this entire concept of the use of "Lord" to indicate an intact relationship with God can be found by a broader study

---

[71] Berlin and Brettler, *Jewish Study Bible*, 328.

[72] Prager, *Rational Study Bible*, 32.

[73] Kenneth Barker, *The NIV Study Bible* (Grand Rapids: Zondervan, 1985), 223.

of who it is who addresses the prophets. If you go through the 12 Minor Prophets, for example, you will discover that it is the "Lord" and not "God" who addresses them on every single occasion. Furthermore, the prophets quote what the "Lord" says or declares, and never once is it stated that the message is from "God." Indeed, there is only one place in which "God" even speaks to the 12 prophets, and this is to the one errant prophet, Jonah. Exactly as with Balaam, the disobedience of Jonah is followed by the appearance of "God" who unpleasantly gains Jonah's attention (Jonah 4:7–9). This is in sharp contrast to the 11 obedient prophets to whom the "Lord" always relates.

The involvement of "the angel of the Lord" with the donkey has the same explanation that has previously been given for this person, and the second person of the Trinity is indicated. Indeed, the Lord himself is immediately at hand as is shown in Numbers 22:27 & 31. Since it is the Lord who opens the donkey's mouth, it appears to be the Lord who is trying to get through to Balaam through the donkey. Indeed, the donkey speaks three sentences, all of which are questions!

Taken together, **Guideline #2** applies to this passage with Balaam, and it appears that it is the second person of the Trinity who is primarily or solely involved.

14. Taking Possession of the Promised Land—Joshua 1–12

Moses dies at the end of Deuteronomy and Joshua takes over leadership of the nation. The book of Joshua opens with the Lord directing Joshua to get Israel into the Promised Land, and this is accomplished by the end of chapter 4. However, a fundamental problem is immediately encountered and it is that Canaanites are living throughout the land in many cities and villages. Further, the sin of the Canaanites was notable even before Abraham and his family moved to Egypt (Genesis 15:16), and by the time the Israelites returned, the Canaanites had multiple gods and they practiced child sacrifice, religious prostitution, divination, and idolatry.[74] Clearly, they were entrenched in the land and in their sinful practices. If the Israelites go into the land with the Canaanites still there, the probability

---

[74] Barker, *NIV Study Bible*, 28.

that their gods will be embraced by the Jews is 100% as shown later and as reported in Judges. How can the land become a spiritually viable place for the people of Israel?

The Lord has the answer, and the answer is to conquer the land. In Joshua 5, the commander of the army of the Lord appears in bodily form to Joshua with a drawn sword in his hand. He announces that he is the commander of the Lord's army, and he requires Joshua to take off his sandals as the ground is holy. Joshua does so, falls down and worships him, and it is clear that he will be taking orders from this commander.

> **Joshua 5:13–15**
>
> Now when Joshua was near Jericho, he looked up and saw a man standing in front of him with a drawn sword in his hand. Joshua went up to him and asked, "Are you for us or for our enemies?" "Neither," he replied, "but as commander of the army of the Lord I have now come." Then Joshua fell facedown to the ground in reverence, and asked him, "What message does my Lord have for his servant?" The commander of the Lord's army replied, "Take off your sandals, for the place where you are standing is holy." And Joshua did so.

The conquering of the Promised Land begins under the Lord's direction in Joshua 6. This begins with the destruction of Jericho and the killing of all the people except for Rahab and her household (Joshua 6:22–23). Despite Achan's sin (chapter 7) and the Gibeonite deception (chapter 9), the conquering proceeds city by city until 31 kings and their people are destroyed (Joshua 12:24).

Throughout the conquering, all people and animals are killed. Just as he did to Pharaoh in Egypt (Exodus 4:21), the Lord hardened the hearts of the peoples so that they did not seek to make peace with Israel and were therefore ultimately destroyed (Joshua 11:19–20). Even though not complete, the conquering stopped for a period when Joshua was very old (Joshua 13:1–5). While there was some additional conquering after the death of Joshua (see Judges 1), soon the people of Israel were worshipping the gods of the Canaanites who still lived in the land (Judges 2:10–13). The result was a hugely negative period with major sinful times between the judges which God sent.

The Lord rather than God gives Joshua instructions through the book of Joshua with all of the conquering which took place. Further, the roles and speech of the Lord (**Keys #2 & 3**) are very similar to those of the second person of the Trinity in the New Testament. Thus, **Guideline #2** applies and the second person of the Trinity is indicated as "the Lord" through Joshua 1–12.

PAUSE

The mass killings make this one of the most difficult passages of all in the entire Old Testament. Even the sword in Joshua 5:13 is troubling, especially as it is drawn and ready for use. To make matters worse, our guidelines and all our keys unquestionably point to the conclusion that it is the second person of the Trinity who is in charge. Why is all of this such a problem for many of us when it is not at all clear that this section of scripture has been so unpalatable through the history of Christianity? Here are three possible reasons for this:

First, I believe that our views of scripture relate to the era of time in which we live. More than 100 years ago, for example, God's authority was more likely to be accepted without question. In 1563 and in reference to this section of scripture, John Calvin pointed out that life and death are in the hands of God, and that since God justly doomed the Canaanites to destruction, this "ends all discussion."[75] In his 1708 commentary, Matthew Henry said that with their unrighteousness, the people of Canaan had forfeited their lives, and that therefore we should not entertain any thought of God being unrighteous in handing down this sentence.[76] Perhaps we are more sensitive to efforts to exterminate whole groups of people such as with Hitler and the Jews which resulted in the word "genocide."[77] Regardless, I think it likely that in our era of time we are less willing to accept the absolute authority of the divine.

Second, I believe that how we feel about the destruction of the Canaanites depends upon where we live, our geographical location. If

---

[75] John Calvin, *Commentaries on the Book of Joshua* (Grand Rapids: Baker Books, 2005), 97. Reprint of the 1563 original.

[76] Matthew Henry. *Matthew Henry's Commentary on the Whole Bible* vol. 2 (Old Tappan, NJ: F. H. Revell Company, no date), 32. Reprint of the 1708 original.

[77] David B. Guralnik, ed., *Webster's New World Dictionary* (New York: Simon & Schuster, 1982), 582.

we live in an area in which there is great sensitivity to social injustice, this portion of scripture is likely to disturb us more. In the United States, for example, social injustice issues are focused in the urban areas much more than in the rural regions. Demonstrations are in cities, not in the country, and this is not just because there are more people in metropolitan areas but because people seem actually to think differently there. Voting patterns certainly show this, and perhaps even our views of scripture are also influenced by the subcultures in which we live.

Third, I believe that how we respond to the killings in Joshua correlates with the churches we attend. If you attend a church with a focus upon Jesus and your relationship with him, you are not as likely to be disturbed by the killings in Joshua perhaps because relationships among people are less likely to be the focus of your thinking in spiritual areas. Instead, the focus is more likely to be upon sin, upon the Savior, upon the cross, and upon obedience to Jesus. But, if you attend a church with a primary focus upon relationships between people including social justice issues, you are much more likely to be disturbed by the book of Joshua, and it is extremely difficult to see Jesus there. In such churches, people expect Jesus to have the same social justice focus as they have, to be nonviolent, and to be taking steps to resolve social justice issues by promoting love, peace, and the acceptance of everyone. Scriptures tend to be interpreted so that they do not distract from this social justice emphasis.[78]

What I find to be of interest about these three points is that they are situational with major influences upon scriptural interpretations connected to eras of time, geographical locations, and church affiliations. Should not scriptural content be the determining factor here? Our situations are

---

[78] When Jesus made a whip and drove the money changers out of the temple in John 2:13-16, it is possible to interpret this as nonviolent because it is not clear that Jesus actually struck anyone. Likewise, when he said he came not to bring peace but a sword in Matthew 10:34, one can call the sword merely a figure of speech. When Jesus advocated buying a sword in Luke 22:36, it can be said that this was for defense and not for any offensive action. And, when Jesus is pictured as having a sword coming out of his mouth in Revelation 1:16, this can be seen as a visual picture of the word of God. Other like scriptures can be interpreted in similar ways with the result that Jesus can be seen as a nonviolent purveyor of love, peace, and social justice. The mass killings reported in Joshua 1-12 are incompatible with this viewpoint, of course, and therefore, Jesus cannot be seen as associated with them.

transient, but the word of our God stands forever (Isaiah 40:8; 1 Peter 1:25).

I have been able to gain peace in this entire area by focusing upon the scriptures that tell us how to respond to God's authority such as Isaiah 29:16, Jeremiah 18:1–10, and Romans 9:14–24. This focus has allowed me to come to grips as best as possible with the killings that occurred in order to make the Promised Land spiritually habitable for the people of Israel. Fully facing the difficult teachings in the New Testament has also been of value to me in giving me a broader perspective. It is my hope that you as a reader can also come to grips with these difficult scriptures, and that you can do so without feeling that it is impossible for the second person of the Trinity to have been involved.

---

15. Gideon—Judges 6–7

The period of the judges follows Joshua and this was a most difficult time as the people of Israel began worshipping the gods of the unconquered peoples around them. As a result, they were handed over to raiders who plundered them (Judges 2:14). Judges 2 summarizes many of the problems at that time, and it also indicates that the Lord repeatedly raised up judges to rescue the nation. Again and again, the Lord was with the judges and things got better, but when the judges died, things got even worse than before with disobedience and the worship of other gods (Judges 2:16–19).

Gideon was one of the judges, and in Judges 6 we have an interesting account of a divine person visiting him. The person is initially called "the angel of the Lord" in verse 11, but by verse 14, the name is merely "the Lord." As indicated earlier, this subtle change supports the contention that "the angel of the Lord" really means "the Lord." Gideon is addressed as "mighty warrior" in verse 12 even though it is out of fear that he is threshing wheat in a highly confined space so that the Midianites would not come and take it. The conversation that follows between the Lord and Gideon is of great interest including a question asked by the Lord in verse 14. The question, "Am I not sending you?" really conveys information rather than being a question to be answered, just as are many of the questions which Jesus asks in the gospels.

In Judges 6:22, Gideon clearly recognizes that he is talking to the divine face to face and yet he has survived. Of course, he is talking with the Lord and not with God, and the Lord assures him in verse 23 that Gideon will not die. Gideon tears down the altar to Baal, he is in trouble immediately with the local population, and the Midianites and other enemies assemble in a great army. In all of this, **Guideline #2** applies and **Keys #2 & 3** provide solid support that it is the second person of the Trinity who is at work in this passage.

While the Lord is consistently involved in the first 35 verses of Judges 6, the situation abruptly changes in verse 36. Confronted with what appears to be the impossible assignment of leading the people of Israel to crush their enemies, Gideon addresses "God," not "Lord," and asks him to provide two signs for him. God did so (verses 38 and 40) in apparent recognition of Gideon's human need for assurance. However, God's verbal response to Gideon is truly interesting because it represents the ultimate in conciseness—zero words. Clearly, **Guideline #1** applies to this portion of the passage.

The story continues in Judges 7 where the Lord comes back and directs Gideon in a most interesting and decisive "battle" in which it is the Lord who makes the Midianites turn on each other and the result is victory for Israel. **Guideline #2** again applies and **Keys #2 & 3** are supportive of the second person of the Trinity at work. Overall, it clear that both the first and the second persons of the Trinity are involved in this interesting story of Gideon.

16. Samson's Parents—Judges 13

Again the people of Israel did evil in the sight of the Lord and the Lord delivered them into the hands of the Philistines for 40 years. However, truly characteristic of his love for his people, in Judges 13 the angel of the Lord appeared first to a childless woman and then later to her husband and her together. They were given specific instructions about a boy who was to be born to them and who would redeem Israel as one of the judges. Both parents believed the angel of the Lord and offered a burnt offering to the Lord.

There is much evidence that the angel of the Lord appeared in bodily form to the parents of Samson on the two occasions indicated. It was not in a ghost-like or visionary form but a bodily presentation and a meal was offered him. The interactions were extended and truly conversational, and there was one question asked by the angel of the Lord (Judges 13:18). Manoah, the father to be, was convinced that they had seen God and that as a consequence they would die (Judges 13:22). His wife, however, gave him some solid reasons why this would not occur. One cannot expect Manoah to have an understanding of the Trinity, and thus, he did not distinguish between "God" and "Lord" (or, "the angel of the Lord"). Just as in the New Testament where there is no evidence that anyone ever saw the first person of the Trinity face to face, there is no evidence for a similar sighting here. Instead, it is reasonable to conclude that once again, as in the New Testament, these people saw the second person of the Trinity face to face. Yes, they saw the divine, but not God the Father. **Guideline #2** applies to this passage and **Keys #2 & 3** are supportive.

17. Call of Samuel—1 Samuel 3

Samuel was born following a miraculous conception and as a very young boy, his mother, Hannah, gave him up for service in the temple in Jerusalem under the priest Eli. But Eli did not meet the expectations of the Lord and his sons were wicked. A man of God told Eli of the doom that was to come to his house and that a "faithful priest" was to take Eli's place (1 Samuel 2:27–36). Clearly, this priest was to be Samuel. In a well-known story, the Lord calls the boy Samuel three times in one night, but Samuel did not yet know the Lord (1 Samuel 3:7) and he incorrectly thinks that it is Eli calling him. Eli then realizes that it is the Lord who is calling Samuel, and he tells Samuel how to respond. The Lord called the boy a fourth time, and this time they connected and a message was delivered to Samuel. It is truly touching that the Lord came in bodily form to be with the boy Samuel, and to communicate with him personally (1 Samuel 3:10). This reminds us of the most tender actions that Jesus demonstrated towards children in the New Testament where he placed his hands on them and prayed for them (Matthew 19:13–15). **Guideline #2** applies to this passage and **Keys #2 & 3** are supportive of the second person of the Trinity being the deity here.

18. Testing of Job—Job 1:6–2:10

We now come to two passages in the book of Job which are far different from anything else we have covered. In both of these passages (Job 1:6–12; 2:1–10), the Lord confronts Satan directly and taunts him with the righteousness of Job. Job's righteousness absolutely flies in the face of everything Satan stands for. In effect, the Lord tells Satan that Job is godly and that Satan cannot do a thing about it. Satan responds by saying that if Job's good fortune is taken away from him, he will crumble and curse God. But the Lord says no, that will not happen, and he gives Satan the chance to prove his point. Satan jumps at the chance to prove the Lord wrong and the book of Job swings into high gear.

We could comment at great length on this entire long book, including Job's reactions to terrible adversity, the extended remarks of his friends, and Job's responses to those remarks. However, to keep ourselves on track, we should note that the only divine person speaking in Job is the Lord, and thus we must apply **Guideline #2**. Turning to **Key #2**, whether the Lord is a "mediator" in this situation could be debated, but he is certainly in charge and he is the divine person at hand who is connecting with other beings even though they are not humans. The application of **Key #3** reveals two conversations with Satan, both of which are kicked off by questions. Thus, while not lengthy, the speech of the Lord is consistent with what we would expect from the second person of the Trinity. Overall, considering all factors, it is believed that the second person of the Trinity is the person to whom "Lord" refers in the passage at hand.

19. Questioning of Job—Job 38–41

After all the speeches of Job's friends and his multiple responses to them, we have the culminating messages from the Lord. In these four chapters, the Lord asks Job the most penetrating questions imaginable. In chapter 38 alone, he asks 34 questions in 41 verses! In fact he asks 70 questions altogether in the four chapters, and this is the greatest concentration of questions in the entire Bible.

The Lord starts in chapter 38 with questions pertaining to creation, and he uses the word "I" indicating that he had a personal hand in creation. If we did not know that this was true for the second person of the Trinity, this would push us towards the conclusion that the first person of the Trinity is the speaker. However, we know that the second person of the Trinity was vitally involved in creation (John 1:1–3; Colossians 1:16; Hebrews 1:3). It was by him that *all things* were created. Thus, it is entirely appropriate that the second person uses "I" in this passage.

The Lord then goes on to demonstrate his divinity by asking many questions to which only the divine can adequately respond. As a whole, these are rhetorical questions used to teach and drive home points, and one is reminded of how Jesus taught in the gospels. Many of his questions there had similar objectives, and yes, questions were often asked back to back.

There is one other point here, and it is that in each case where the Lord referred to God (Job 38:33 & 41; 39:17; 40:2 & 19), he spoke of God in the third person. For example, he spoke of "God's dominion over the earth," how young animals "cry out to God," how "God did not endow" certain animals with wisdom, how anyone who accuses God should answer to God, and how the behemoth "ranks first among the works of God" (Job 40:19). He does not say, "*My* dominion over the earth" or "young animals cry out to *me*." These observations do not support a contention that the speaker is God the Father.

In sum, **Guideline #2** applies because the only identified speaker is "the Lord." With regard to **Key #2**, the Lord makes extreme efforts to connect Job with God and to get Job to understand what the will of God is. This, of course, is exactly what Jesus did with us. As for **Key #3**, the speech of the Lord is extended rather than concise, it is at least somewhat conversational, and it employs an extensive use of questions. Taken together, the conclusion is drawn that the second person of the Trinity is "the Lord" in this lengthy passage.

20. The Lord Our Shepherd—Psalm 23

This psalm is highly valued by Jews and Christians alike. Starting the psalm with "The Lord" unquestionably gets the psalm off on the right foot as it implies a personal connection with people. While there is power in "Lord," the focus of the name is not on the presence of absolute power such as is indicated by "God." Instead, the focus is on the relationship with the divine, a relationship which is truly enhanced by "my shepherd."

"My" underscores the connectedness here, for the author claims a personal relationship with the divine. Further, the fact that the divine person is pictured as a shepherd makes the author (and us) the sheep, and there is no doubt about who is in charge. Sheep do not argue with their shepherd.

The shepherd pictured here is a good shepherd, one who cares for his sheep and who meets their needs, including spiritual ones, such as by guiding them in paths of righteousness. The shepherd keeps his people from being fearful, even in the worst possible circumstances of life. He provides ongoing comfort, keeps his people from anyone who would demean them, provides the personal touch of blessing, and offers eternal love. Who can do such things? In the New Testament, Jesus clearly gives the answer by saying, "I am the good shepherd" and then by going on to tell what this really means including the voluntary laying down his life for his sheep (John 10:11–18).

Psalm 23 is unlike any of the others that we have considered in our studies because it does not include even one word said by a deity. Thus, there is no information for **Key #3**. However, the Lord's role as a mediator and caretaker is well spelled out (**Key #2**), and all Christians know who the Lord is in this Psalm. Clearly, **Guideline #2** applies.

21. When "God" is "Lord"—Isaiah 53

We move on to the prophets, and several passages are selected for study. Isaiah 53 is especially relevant as it is the best recognized prophecy of the coming of Jesus in the entire Old Testament. While our focus is not on prophecy, within Isaiah 53 we have a reminder that "Lord" sometimes does in fact refer to God the Father in the Old Testament, just as it did in

> **Isaiah 53—Selected verses**
>
> 1. Who has believed our message and to whom has the arm of the Lord been revealed?
> 4. Surely he took up our pain and bore our suffering...
> 6. We all, like sheep, have gone astray, each of us has turned to our own way; and the Lord has laid on him the iniquity of us all.
> 10. Yet it was the Lord's will to crush him and cause him to suffer...

the New Testament. As "Lord" is the name for the divine in this passage, **Guideline #2** applies, but we know right away that we will need additional contextual information, including **Keys #2 & 3** in order to determine if the reference is to the first or the second person of the Trinity.

While it is not necessarily clear to which member of the Trinity "Lord" refers to in verse 1, it is clear that this is God the Father by the time one gets to verse 6. The contextual information here is compelling, and the role of the Lord can only be that of God the Father. **Key #2** is therefore useful, but **Key #3** is not helpful as there is no speech by the divine. Of course, **Key #3** is not needed because the conclusion as to which person of the Trinity is involved is absolutely clear.

22. Call of Jeremiah—Jeremiah 1

The call of the prophets is routinely done by the Lord, and sometimes the call is especially touching. Beginning with Jeremiah 1:4, there is one of the most touching calls of all, especially considering the huge adversities that Jeremiah will face during his life as a prophet. The Lord comes to Jeremiah, says that he knew him before he was formed in the womb, and asserts that before Jeremiah was born, he was set apart as a prophet. When Jeremiah indicates his inadequacy, the Lord assures him verbally, but then does more by reaching out and actually touching Jeremiah. So yes, the Lord must have been physically present. As it is our Lord Jesus Christ who is the only member of the Trinity who we are certain who has ever assumed a physical body, who else can it be in this passage? And then, in verse 11, the content of the book right after the call is initiated with (you guessed it) a question! **Guideline #2** applies, and all information is supportive of the second person of the Trinity being the "Lord."

23. Four Men in the Fiery Furnace—Daniel 3

We now examine the most unusual of all of the 25 passages selected for study, unusual because in contrast to all the other passages, the initial impression is that very little information is available for any of our keys. This should not disqualify this passage for inclusion, however, because our sole criterion for inclusion is a "general agreement that the divine is at work" (page 82). Indeed, there would be such agreement because of the miracles that happened when three godly men are thrown bound into a fiery furnace. The fourth man found walking around with them quickly becomes the focus, and we are compelled to ask who that man is.

First, based upon a standard translation such as the NIV, we have one clue as to who the fourth man is, and that is from the remark of the king upon looking into the furnace: "Look! I see four men walking around in the fire, unbound and unharmed, and the fourth looks like a son of the gods." (Daniel 3:25). The Hebrew is faithfully rendered as "a son of the gods," so there is no problem there, but one wonders where the king got his words to describe the fourth man. For us as Christians, it is easy to read "Son of God" into his words, but he did not exactly say that, and neither "God" or "Lord" is to be found anywhere here.

In tough cases like this, I routinely turn to *The Jewish Study Bible* which presents the Tanakh translation. It reports the king as saying, "… the fourth looks like a divine being."[79] For Christians this would point to one of the members of the Trinity, but in the marginal notes, the editors clearly indicate what the Jews will almost always say in such a situation, and this is that the person at hand is an angel. You see, if you believe that there is just one God and that God is indivisible and cannot be seen, you will not believe that God will appear physically to people. However, God can send a messenger who is an angel. If you agree with this, you will be led in a very different direction than if you say the fourth man is a member of the Trinity.

When we turn from the Hebrew to the LXX, we get a great deal more information. There are more details about the event, and there are two long prayers of praise to God given by the men in the furnace. In fact, there are actually 100 verses in Daniel 3 in the Theodotion LXX manuscript rather than 30 in the Hebrew. Concerning the fourth man, the LXX plainly states that "the angel of the Lord" came down into the furnace to be with the men and to change the hot air into a "moist breeze."[80] This provided such relief to the men that they uttered a prayer of blessing to the Lord which was some 39 verses long. At the end of this, the king observed the fourth man and pronounced that he was "like a divine son." If you accept the LXX and the statement that "the angel of the Lord" came down, it

---

[79] Berlin and Brettler, *Jewish Study Bible*, 1648.
[80] Pietersma and Wright (eds.), *New English Translation of the Septuagint*, 1001-03.

is much clearer that Christ did that whereas the Hebrew simply does not provide that information.

In terms of our second key which pertains to the role of the divine person in this story, one can infer from both the Hebrew and the Greek that it was to comfort and support the three men, but the Greek more clearly shows this. Such a role is within the role of the second person of the Trinity. Nothing can be obtained from our third key as there is no recorded speech of the fourth man either in the Hebrew or in the Greek.

Overall, there are definite hints in the Hebrew that the second person of the Trinity is the fourth man, but "the angel of the Lord" identification in the LXX establishes this conclusion much more clearly. **Key #2** supports this even though no information from **Key #3** is available. As a result, the criteria for **Guideline #2** are met and the conclusion is drawn that the fourth man in the fiery furnace is the second person of the Trinity.

24. Daniel in the Den of Lions—Daniel 6

"God" is mentioned no fewer than 10 times in this chapter of 28 verses, and the king in the story shows great reverence for God. After Daniel's night with the lions, the king approaches him in the morning and inquiries about his welfare. Daniel responds, "My God sent his angel, and he shut the mouths of the lions" (Daniel 6:21). The wording here does not include "the angel of the Lord" and it does not include the word "Lord" either. The divine person involved is simply referred to as "God" throughout the passage. Thus, we can conclude that **Guideline #1** applies and that the first person of the Trinity is involved by sending an angel to keep Daniel safe.

25. The Call of the Twelve Prophets—Hosea through Malachi

As table 2 in chapter 3 shows (page 14), the group of 12 prophets with shorter writings (thus the term "minor") has simply been called "The Twelve" by Jewish people over the ages. The grouping of these together may have been facilitated by the fact that all 12 of these short books will fit on a single scroll. The LXX, however, recognized each book separately in its reorganization of the Old Testament scriptures, and Christians have followed the LXX.

In terms of our studies, what stands out is that the "Lord" is quoted within the first few verses of every one of the 12 books. Near the start of each book, the text most commonly says something such as, "The word of the Lord that came to ..." and then the prophet's name is given. When this is not done, the Lord is quoted in the next few verses and in all cases it is clear that the message to be conveyed comes from the Lord. He is mentioned more than 500 times in these 12 short books. In no case is it indicated that the message is from God even though there are references to God made throughout the texts.

The 12 books routinely contain judgments against Israel, punishments, and promises of better times in the future with improved obedience to God. Among the 12 prophets, it is Jonah who is clearly disobedient, going the opposite way after receiving the command from the Lord to go to Nineveh. Furthermore, he returns only reluctantly, and he is angry when the Lord shows compassion to the gentiles. It must have been quite a sight as he sat outside the city of Nineveh waiting for it to be destroyed, furiously angry. Beginning with Jonah 4:7, "God" is mentioned twice as acting in the situation (providing the worm and the scorching wind). "God" even asks Jonah a question: "Is it right for you to be angry about the plant?" (Jonah 4:9). The explanation for "God" being included in the text, instead of "Lord," is the same as it was for Balaam—the covenant relationship was broken and the writer was therefore unwilling to use "Lord" because it would imply an intact relationship. If that explanation is accurate, it was not God who spoke with Jonah and asked the question, but the Lord. Sadly, it is not clear that Jonah ever repented and this book does not end on a positive note.

The overall conclusion from this section on the 12 Minor Prophets is that it is the second person of the Trinity who speaks God's will to these prophets, and who tells them what to say and do. **Guideline #2** clearly applies, and confirmation is provided by **Keys #2 & 3**.

Conclusions from the Studies of Old Testament Passages

Before we list the conclusions that can be reasonably drawn from our studies in the Old Testament, we need to remind ourselves of the limitations of our efforts. Clearly, we could not study the whole Old Testament, and not even all passages where there would be general agreement that the divine was at work. Further, we were not able to study hundreds of cases in which "God" and "Lord" appeared with little or no contextual information. It is hoped that these portions of the Old Testament can be included in future studies where they may render additional information. However, if they could be included, it would appear that their inclusion would add to and not take away from the findings of our studies on the detailed passages.

Many of the findings from the 25 passages are summarized in table 6 (pages 84-86). These studies really constituted a test of each of the three keys and each of the three guidelines to see whether they would hold up, even though they were developed on the basis of the New Testament. Here is a summary of the conclusions which can reasonably be drawn overall:

- **Key #1—Enduring names for God**. A fundamental contention through this book is that the enduring names for God through the Bible are two: "God" and "Lord." This key received strong support from our Old Testament studies since one or the other of these names or both were found in all 25 passages if one willing to accept the LXX for #23—Four Men in the Fiery Furnace. Sometimes, "the angel of the …" was added to "Lord," but few other variations were observed. Exactly as in the New Testament, "God" was routinely associated with the first person of the Trinity and "Lord" was typically, but not always, associated with the second person of the Trinity.

- **Key #2—Primary roles of the divine**. Based on the New Testament, the primary roles for "God" and "Lord," as summarized in table 4 (page 65), were applied to the Old Testament passages. In just one case (#18—Testing of Job), the role of the divine could not be clearly discerned. However, in the other 24 cases, the roles of "God" and "Lord" all agreed with the final judgment as to which member of the Trinity was involved. Overall, a remarkable consistency was found across the testaments between the primary roles demonstrated and membership in the Trinity.

- **Key #3—Speech patterns of the divine**. In 20 of 25 cases, the speech patterns of the first and second members of the Trinity in the Old Testament were in agreement with the conclusion as to which member of the Trinity was actually involved. However, in five cases, no speech was recorded for the member of the Trinity in the passage and thus the speech patterns key could not be applied. Also, the first member of the Trinity spoke on four especially important occasions ("landmark communications"), and in each case he spoke in the expected way, although longer than anticipated. The greater length is no doubt due to the importance of the occasions, but the longer narrations were not anticipated because there are no New Testament parallels. Overall, **Key #3** was definitely of value, but not quite as consistently as **Keys #1 & 2**, primarily because the divine did not always speak.

- **Guideline #1—"God" is used alone or with another name other than "Lord."** Using the rules for this guideline given in table 5 (page 78), this guideline held up except for two cases (Balaam and Jonah), where "God" instead of "Lord" had likely been inserted in the text by the writer due to the breaking of the covenant by these prophets. If one can accept this explanation, the guideline holds up perfectly.

- **Guideline #2—"Lord" is used alone or with another name other than "God."** As outlined in table 5, this guideline was concordant with the final conclusion in every case.

- **Guideline #3—"God" and "Lord" used together in one way or another**. The passages called for this guideline only twice, but in each case the result was concordant with the final conclusion drawn as to which member of the Trinity was involved.

- **Overall findings—First member of the Trinity**. In seven of the 25 passages studied, it was the first person of the Trinity who was the divine person involved, and in an additional two cases, he was involved with the second person of the Trinity. Routinely, he was called "God." He assumed the roles of being creator, founder, director, administrator, and the one who sets down all parameters and makes the covenants. These roles were consistent across the testaments. In characteristic form, the first person came and efficiently did what he needed to do. Consequently, his work was presented crisply and succinctly with only about five chapters being required altogether to present his work in the seven passages where he was the sole deity.

- **Overall findings—Second member of the Trinity.** In 16 of the 25 passages studied, it was the second person of the Trinity who was the divine person involved. There were two additional cases in which he was definitely involved with the first person of the Trinity. Routinely, he was called "Lord" through his appearances. A prominent feature here is the connections he made with people as he conveyed the will of God. At least some of these contacts were made personally and face-to-face. In general, the roles of the second person of the Trinity in the Old Testament were very similar to his roles in the New Testament. However, the 16 Bible portions in which he was found consumed a huge amount of space in the Old Testament (approximately 178 chapters).[81]

- **Contributions of the LXX.** The LXX made major contributions to an understanding of three of the 25 passages (#4—Noah and the Ark; #8—Preparation for the Covenant with Moses; #23—Four Men in the Fiery Furnace). Indeed, without the LXX, these passages would have stood outside the system of understanding of the presence and work of members of the Trinity propounded in this volume. The LXX promoted seeing similarities in the names, roles, and communication patterns of the first and second members of the Trinity across the testament. Given the information presented about the LXX in chapter 3, a reasonable approach for its use is to lay it side by side with the Hebrew text as one reads and interprets passages in the Old Testament. Both are thereby considered authoritative, but one or the other may be especially helpful in the understanding of any particular Old Testament passage.

The studies reported in this chapter lead to the overriding conclusion that the second person of the Trinity is actively involved in numerous

---

[81] Note is made that for matters of convenience, the 12 minor prophets were grouped together. However, one could easily argue that they should be considered separately, and if so, the second person of the Trinity is the sole divine person in not 16 of 25 sections of scripture studied but in 27 of 36.

places in the Old Testament. His involvement with people bears striking similarities to his involvement with people in the New Testament, and he is a mediator between God and people repeatedly in the Old Testament. Even his speech is similar to his speech in the New Testament as it is frequently conversational and with a prominence of questions. It was further found that "God" and "Lord" are indeed the enduring names for God through the Old Testament just as they are in the New Testament. The unity of scriptures is therefore clearly in evidence.

Note is made that our findings regarding the frequent appearances of Christ in the Old Testament are highly compatible with the beliefs of Justin Martyr, Tertullian, Calvin, Walvoord, and Murray as briefly summarized in the Preface (page xi). Our studies, however, have been very different than those of these authors, and it is hoped that the approach taken here will be found to be convincing and not easy to dismiss. If so, the common appearance of the topic of Christ in the Old Testament in theological studies will be promoted, and this will certainly be a step forward in a more in-depth understanding of our Lord Jesus Christ.

Six

Conclusions, Implications, and a Challenge

Let us now succinctly summarize our entire study and the conclusions we have drawn from it. We will then go on to identify the implications of our study, and finally to explore one of the challenges for the future to which all of this leads.

Study Summary and Conclusions

The gospels clearly show that Jesus has a profound interest in people and their welfare, and his devotion to them is so marked that he gave up his life for them. Further, his nature is unchanging across the eons of time (Hebrews 13:8). How can these facts be compatible with the position that most Christians hold, namely, that since the creation of the world, Jesus came to earth and walked with people for only one period of time, his incarnation? If he cares so much for people, wouldn't he have found a way to be with people frequently such as during Old Testament times, connecting with them and caring for them?

This book has squarely addressed the fundamental question at hand by a systematic and a quantitative study of the relevant portions of scripture which point to the presence and work of the first and second persons of the Trinity. Three variables were found which clearly differentiated the first and second persons of the Trinity in the New Testament. These variables were called **"Keys"** and they were then found to also be effective in the Old Testament in making this distinction. They are as follows:

- **Key #1—Enduring names for God.** "God" and "Lord" were shown to be the enduring names for God throughout the Bible. The single name "God" routinely refers to the first person of the Trinity and "Lord" typically, but not always, refers to the second person of the Trinity. These rules hold for both the Old and the New Testaments. While the two words can be used interchangeably, differences in meaning in the Bible are clearly documented in our studies, and those differences are especially helpful in sorting out whether the first or second person of the Trinity is at work.

- **Key #2—Primary roles of the divine.** As creator, founder, and administrator, the first person of the Trinity sets the parameters, makes the rules, and establishes the covenants. The overarching primary role of the second person is as a mediator between God and people. His focus upon people is marked and he repeatedly conveys to people truths about God including God's will and love for the human race. These roles hold throughout both testaments, and they help to earmark the person of the Trinity who is at work in numerous scriptural passages.

- **Key #3—Speech patterns of the divine.** The speech patterns of the first and second persons of the Trinity were systematically studied. The first person is concise, he uses declarative sentences in laying down principles and instructions, and he does not ask questions. The second person of the Trinity directs his speech towards people, his communications are often conversational, and a favorite verbal tool of his is that of using questions. These speech patterns hold for both the Old and New Testaments.

Some easy to apply **Guidelines** were set up which were based upon the three keys and which allowed us to find and to distinguish between God the Father and God the Son in the New Testament. With the validity of the guidelines established in the New Testament, they were then applied to 25 sections of scripture in the Old Testament where they were found to be just as effective in distinguishing between the first and second persons of the Trinity.

In our studies, the **Septuagint (LXX)** proved to be of major assistance in more fully understanding the intricacies of the Old Testament. The value of its use in a parallel way with the Hebrew Masoretic text was clearly documented, and uncertainties in one text can frequently be clarified by the other. It is hoped that the contributions of the LXX will be more broadly accepted in the future than has been the case in the past, and making the LXX readily available in English and in other languages in the standard Old Testament form would assist greatly in making comparisons with the Hebrew text. Indeed, a side-by-side presentation of the LXX along with a well recognized English Old Testament translation would be ideal.[82]

Finally, the **unity of the scriptures** was repeatedly underscored in our studies. The same primary names for God are found from Genesis to Revelation, and the meanings of "God" and "Lord" remain constant as well. In addition, the roles of the first and second persons of the Trinity are remarkably similar in both testaments. Finally, the very ways in which the first and second persons express themselves are strikingly consistent across the testaments.

In short, our study provided evidence for multiple appearances of the second person of the Trinity throughout the Old Testament. Routinely, these appearances were in connection with people, and it is clear that Christ related to people in a variety of ways including face-to-face encounters. In these meetings, he routinely demonstrated love and caring for his people, and he was with the leaders of Israel on many occasions as they faced struggles in their leadership roles.

Implications

While our entire study and its conclusions can be summarized rather succinctly, the implications are substantial.

---

[82] No side-by-side editions of a standard English translation of the standard Old Testament and the LXX are known to your author. The LXX Old Testament books are available in English interspersed with multiple associated apocryphal writings in Pietersma and Wright (eds.), *New English Translation of the Septuagint.* A useful alternative is to employ an interlinear Greek/English translation such as that of Charles Van der Pool, *The Apostolic Bible Polyglot* (Newport OR: Apostolic Press, 1996). A number of related supportive materials are available through https://www.apostolicbible.com/newstore.html.

- **We need to see our Savior in a new light.** If we think of Jesus almost solely in terms of his incarnation, we will miss some real depths of his nature. Our systematic and careful study of scripture has shown that from of Garden of Eden onward, he has come to earth to be with people time and time again, talking with them, walking with them, and providing guidance for them. For thousands of years, he has served as a mediator and has drawn people closer to God on numerous occasions. Even when the people of Israel strayed from his commands and worshipped other gods, he continued to care for them, and he will do the same for us.

- **We need to stop putting limitations on our Savior.** We spent an entire chapter on the limitations Christians commonly put on Jesus in terms of where he can be, when he can be there, and what he can teach. These have proven to be blinders because they have kept us from seeing the full depth of his nature, even in the New Testament. Indeed, we reviewed a whole series of teachings of Jesus in the New Testament which are commonly minimized or ignored primarily because they do not sync with twenty-first century western cultural viewpoints. If we were to face and fully accept those teachings in the New Testament, we would find that seeing Jesus in the Old Testament would be much easier because many of the same principles underlie his actions there. Viewing all of these matters in the context of the depth of his love for us will allow us to be led by him like sheep rather than fighting him and the principles he espouses.

- **We need to see the Bible as a truly unified book.** Yes, it consists of two testaments written at different times and by different writers, but there is just one God who is responsible for both. Further, the objective of bringing people to God is the underlying intention of both. The consistencies found across the testaments are stunning, and the Old Testament has uses we rarely think of such as in bringing certain people to Christ. If you have a Jewish friend who expresses an interest in knowing more about Jesus, for example, instead of starting with John 3:16 and Romans 3:23 and 6:23, why not start with scriptures which are likely to be accepted and reverenced? Psalm 23 is a great place to start as it will lead to a discussion of who "the Lord" is. Then, turn to Isaiah 53 and begin to teach about Jesus as Philip did with the Ethiopian in Acts 8. And, on to Psalm 22, Genesis 2, etc. It will become clear to you that you can lead a person to Christ using the Old Testament just as you can with the New Testament.

- **We need to recognize that there are other riches at hand.** For example, we can continue to use "God" and "Lord" interchangeably if we wish, but if we do what the Bible does by distinguishing between these names for God, new depths of meaning will emerge. Open the Bible to anywhere whatsoever, look for "Lord," and ask yourself, "Could this be Jesus?" If after examining the context you are not sure, ask yourself, "Is there any reason why this could not be Jesus?" If you do this with one or two passages a day for a month, it is likely that you will have new knowledge of your Savior because you will have found passages which for the first time you are now convinced do speak of Jesus. A second example of pursuing riches is to put the LXX alongside of your Bible as you read the Old Testament, reading first one and then the other. You may be surprised at the additional understanding you will gain by so doing.

Other implications of our studies could be identified, but as for me, I have in fact been led down one additional line of thinking which I wish to share in the final section of this manuscript.

A Challenge to Further Advance Our Thinking

In this book we have explored the possibility that our Savior was indeed actively involved with people before his incarnation and through Old Testament times. This has been truly broadening, but to push our thinking even farther, what about the period of time since his ascension? Given his enduring nature and his undying commitment to people, is there any chance that he has been involved with people on a rather regular basis since he ascended into heaven?

At first it would seem almost ridiculous to even attempt answering the question at hand. For one thing, Jesus is in heaven, not on the earth, so how can he connect with people on the earth? Further, in his physical absence, he clearly sent the Holy Spirit to provide day-by-day guidance for Christians, so should not our focus be on the third member of the Trinity when we think of the divine? In addition, since by definition we are addressing a period of time which is mostly after the writing of the New Testament, the help that we can expect from that source will certainly be limited.

The reason why this new question is being asked is because we believe that our Savior has shown the highest level of interest in and commitment to people from the Garden of Eden forward. It is his nature to be interested in people and to be utterly devoted to their welfare. Since that is really true, it is <u>not</u> reasonable to assume that this interest simply stopped when he ascended into heaven. Previously, most of us thought little about his involvement with people <u>before</u> his incarnation, so, how about if we think briefly about what he may have been doing with people <u>after</u> his incarnation? No harm in this type of inquiry, and we may find that it also broadens our view of our Savior even further.

There are at least three relevant sources of information which bear on this topic:

1. The New Testament

The New Testament does provide some relevant information. First, let us consider the stoning of Stephen in Acts 7. Stephen first delivered a sermon to the Sanhedrin in which he summarized Jewish history. Then, his voice must have changed and, clearly led by the Holy Spirit, he blasted the Jewish leaders with incredible force (see the text box). The leaders were furious, of course, but the words that follow are of huge significance: **"But Stephen, full of the Holy Spirit, looked up to heaven and saw the glory of God, and**

> **Stephen's Sermon Conclusion (Acts 7:51-52)**
>
> "You stiff-necked people! Your hearts and ears are still uncircumcised. You are just like your ancestors: You always resist the Holy Spirit! Was there ever a prophet your ancestors did not persecute? They even killed those who predicted the coming of the Righteous One. And now you have betrayed and murdered him..."

Jesus standing at the right hand of God. 'Look,' he said, 'I see heaven open and the Son of Man standing at the right hand of God'" (Acts 7:54–56). As they were stoning him, Stephen prayed, **"Lord Jesus, receive my spirit"** (Acts 7:59).

Jesus welcomed Stephen to heaven, there is no doubt about that, and thus Jesus clearly had contact with a human being after he ascended into heaven. Further, in this passage is laid out what Jesus can do for all of us. At first, you may think that because Stephen was a martyr, he is an exceptional case, and the fact that Jesus personally welcomed him to heaven may not be applicable to the rest of us. However, there is no biblical evidence that some saints should be placed at higher levels than others. Indeed, "whoever" believes in Jesus will have eternal life (John 3:16).

Stephen is not the only case of Jesus connecting with people after his ascension into heaven. Acts 9 details the story of Saul's conversion. The Lord speaks from heaven to Saul in an audible voice, and for certain we know it is Jesus because he identifies himself as Jesus in verse 5. Interestingly, the conversation is started with a question from Jesus. Further, a few verses later, the Lord (once again clearly Jesus—see verse 17) has a conversation with Ananias.

The above examples show that after his ascension into heaven, Jesus can and did connect with people on earth. He actually had conversations with them without leaving heaven! Thus, it would be important for us not to fall into the trap of believing that because Jesus is in heaven that he is somehow cut off from people and cannot communicate with them—that is simply not true. That would once again be putting limitations on our Savior.

In addition, there is some evidence from the New Testament for a continuing connection between Jesus and people while he is in heaven. In Hebrews 9:24, for example, it is stated that Jesus entered heaven "...now to appear for us in God's presence." Thus, he represents us before God the Father, and he intercedes for us (Hebrews 7:25). Also, in Hebrews 12:25, we are told that we should not turn away from him "...who warns us from heaven." Thus, he can communicate with us even though he is in heaven.

The above quotes from the New Testament demonstrate that Jesus can connect with people from heaven. They also show that he represents us in heaven, he intercedes for us, and these activities appear to be ongoing.

2. Logic and reason

When you die and go to heaven, who will greet you and welcome you there? It is simply not logical to assume that no one will greet you, that you will find yourself wandering around on the golden streets, trying to get your bearings, and wishing for a GPS. No, it is only logical to believe that you will be greeted and welcomed, and the only question is who will do this? The jokes we hear all assume it will be St. Peter who will greet you at the pearly gates, but is that really likely? You got to heaven because of the sacrifice of one particular person, as a Christian you have committed yourself to that person, and you may well have worked for him for decades. So, logically, who should greet you into your eternal rest?

Clearly, Jesus can do for each of us exactly what he did for Stephen. And, why would he not do this? What a joy it would be for him to connect with those who have committed their lives to him! Would he not want to thank and welcome you as soon as you arrive? And, we could have no greater joy than to meet our Master "face to face" (1 Corinthians 13:12). I believe that he will call each one of us by name when he sees us, a broad smile on his face, and welcome us to heaven. If all of this is correct, Jesus connects with hundreds (or maybe thousands) of people every day as they stream into glory having completed their work on earth. And, perhaps he has done this now for nearly 2,000 years!

These statements seem entirely logical and reasonable. They draw us towards the conclusion that in addition to Jesus being heavily involved with people during Old Testament times and New Testament times, he may very well still be heavily involved with people right now and every day. And, it is not necessary that he have these contacts on earth because he can have contacts in heaven with people as they pass into glory.

3. Death and near-death experiences

There is one more area of human experience which is consistent with what is being proposed here. At the point of death, a number of people become peaceful and exclaim that they see Jesus. Also, there are many near-death experiences which involve a heavenly experience and some with contacts with a divine person recognized as "Jesus." A number of these are summarized in a particular book which reports near-death experiences which have a clear spiritual component.[83] The intention here is merely to introduce this topic.

A single case is presented in order to make the point that Jesus may be involved in a number of near-death experiences, even today. A 22 year old woman was involved in a major motor vehicle accident one night in the Seattle area. She suffered a basal skull fracture, with broken vertebrae in her neck and back. She was taken by ambulance to Harborview Medical Center which is where I worked for more than 30 years. As part of her near-death experience, she felt detached from her body. However, she soon realized that she had someone right next to her, and she immediately recognized that person as Jesus. After the experience was over, she recounted the following:

> *He actually hugged me. He embraced me, and I was very close to him. And I felt his beard and his hair... He actually enveloped me—that's the only word I can think of to describe it. He enveloped me with so much warmth and love... [and his eyes] were piercing eyes. It was like they permeated every part of me, but... not in a mean way. It was like you couldn't lie about anything, and he just looked over and he could see everything. Yet I wanted to reveal everything to him.[84]*

This very positive experience included verbal exchanges with Jesus. Eventually, however, Jesus said that it was not the time for her to pass on and he identified work that she needed yet to do. When he departed, she found herself back in her body, feeling heavy and full of pain.

I have never had a near-death experience, and likely you as a reader have not had one either. However, if you consider a few of these accounts, you will find that it is very difficult to dismiss these experiences. In fact, these reports do raise the possibility that Jesus is even now involved with a number of people near the end of their earthly lives and even on earth.

In sum, the information presented above from the New Testament, from reasoning, and from death and near-death experiences all suggest that

---

[83] John Burke, *Imagine Heaven* (Grand Rapids: Baker Books, 2015).
[84] Burke, *Imagine Heaven*, 34.

Jesus may very well have been rather continuously involved with people since his ascension into heaven. Such involvement would be very consistent with his nature. It is also consistent with the broader idea that Jesus has been involved with people from the Garden of Eden to the present time.

Closing

In closing, it is clear that we cannot limit the appearances of Jesus in time or in the tasks he performs. May we put aside all limitations that we may have unintentionally placed on our Savior, and instead view our Lord Jesus Christ with the broadness and the depth that he deserves. Finally, it is certain that only when we meet him face to face will we truly grasp both his eternal love for people and also his incredible love for each one of us.

Appendix

Detailed Studies of "Lord" in the New Testament

In connection with the studies reported in chapter 5, all New Testament scriptures including the word "Lord"/"Lord's" (NIV, 2011) are listed below according to whether "Lord" definitely or likely refers to the First Person of the Trinity, the Second Person of the Trinity, or whether they are unclassifiable (includes references more difficult to connect with a single member of the Trinity, and also cases of more than one member being involved at the same time).[85]

First Person of the Trinity: God the Father (110 total)

Matthew: 1:20; 1:22; 1:24; 2:13; 2:15; 2:19; 4:7; 4:10; 5:33; 11:25; 21:9; 21:16; 21:42; 22:37; 22:44; 23:39; 28:2

Mark: 11:9; 12:11; 12:29 (2); 12:30; 12:36; 13:20

Luke: 1:6; 1:11; 1:15; 1:16; 1:25; 1:28; 1:32; 1:38; 1:45; 1:46; 1:58; 1:66; 1:68; 2:9 (2); 2:15; 2:22; 2:23 (2); 2:24; 2:29; 2:39; 4:8; 4:12; 4:18; 4:19; 5:17; 10:21; 10:27; 13:35; 19:38; 20:37; 20:42

John: 12:13; 12:38

---

[85] Note is made that all occurrences of "Lord" or "Lord's" in the NIV New Testament (NIV, 2011) are included here except that "Lord's people" put in the place of "saints" on 21 occasions was not included, the reason being that *kurios* was never found in the Greek on those occasions.

Acts: 2:25; 2:34; 2:39; 2:47; 3:19; 3:22; 4:24; 4:26; 4:29; 7:49; 17:24

Romans: 4:8; 9:28; 9:29; 10:16; 11:3; 11:34; 12:19; 14:11

I Corinthians: 14:21

2 Corinthians: 6:17; 6:18

Hebrews: 7:21; 8:2; 8:8; 8:9; 8:10; 8:11; 10:16; 10:30; 12:5; 12:6

James: 1:12; 5:4

2 Peter: 2:11; 3:8; 3:9; 3:15

Revelation: 4:8; 4:11; 11:4; 11:15; 11:17; 15:3; 15:4; 16:7; 18:8; 19:6; 21:22; 22:5; 22:6

Second Person of the Trinity: God the Son (515 total)

Matthew: 3:3; 7:21 (2); 7:22 (2); 8:2; 8:6; 8:8; 8:21; 8:25; 9:28; 9:38; 12:8; 14:28; 14:30; 15:22; 15:25; 15:27; 16:22; 17:4; 17:15; 18:21; 20:30; 20:31; 20:33; 21:3; 22:43; 22:44; 22:45; 24:42; 25:37; 25:44; 26:22

Mark: 1:3; 2:28; 5:19; 7:28; 11:3; 12:36; 12:37; 16:19; 16:20

Luke: 1:43; 1:76; 2:11; 2:26; 3:4; 5:8; 5:12; 6:5; 6:46 (2); 7:6; 7:13; 7:19; 9:54; 9:59; 9:61; 10:1; 10:2; 10:17; 10:39; 10:40; 10:41; 11:1; 11:39; 12:41; 12:42; 13:15; 13:23; 17:5; 17:37; 18:6; 18:41; 19:8 (2); 19:31; 19:34; 20:42; 20:44; 22:33; 22:38; 22:49; 22:61 (2); 24:3; 24:34

John: 1:23; 6:23; 6:68; 9:38; 11:2; 11:3; 11:12; 11:21; 11:27; 11:32; 11:34; 11:39; 12:38; 13:6; 13:9; 13:13; 13:14; 13:25; 13:36: 13:37; 14:5; 14:8; 14:22; 20:2; 20:13; 20:18; 20:20; 20:25; 20:28; 21:7 (2); 21:12; 21:15; 21:16; 21:17; 21:20; 21:21

Acts: 1:6; 1:21; 1:24; 2:20; 2:21; 2:25; 2:34; 2:36; 4:33; 5:14; 7:31; 7:33; 7:59; 7:60; 8:16; 8:22; 8:24; 8:25; 9:1; 9:5; 9:10 (2); 9:11; 9:13; 9:15; 9:17; 9:27 (2); 9:28; 9:31; 9:35; 9:42; 10:4; 10:14; 10:33; 10:36; 11:8; 11:16; 11:17; 11:20; 11:21 (2); 11:23; 11:24; 12:7; 12:11; 12:17; 13:2; 13:10; 13:11; 13:12; 13:44; 13:47; 13:48; 13:49; 14:3; 14:23; 15:11; 15:17 (2); 15:26; 15:35; 15:36; 15:40; 16:14; 16:15; 16:31; 16:32; 18:8; 18:9; 18:25; 19:5; 19:10; 19:13; 19:17; 19:20; 20:19;

20:21; 20:24; 20:35; 21:13; 21:14; 22:8; 22:10 (2); 22:18; 22:19; 22:21; 23:11; 26:15 (2); 28:31

Romans: 1:4; 1:7; 4:24; 5:1; 5:11; 5:21; 6:23; 7:25; 8:39; 10:9; 10:12 (2); 10:13; 12:11; 13:14; 14:4; 14:6 (3) 14:8 (3); 14:9; 14:14; 15:6; 15:11; 15:30; 16:2; 16:8; 16:11; 16:12 (2); 16:13; 16:18; 16:20; 16:22

I Corinthians: 1:2 (2); 1:3; 1:7; 1:8; 1:9; 1:10; 1:31; 2:8; 2:16; 4:4; 4:5; 4:17; 4:19; 5:3; 5:4; 5:5; 6:11; 6:13 (2); 6:14; 6:17; 7:10; 7:12; 7:17; 7:22 (2); 7:25 (2); 7:32 (2); 7:34 (2); 7:35; 7:39; 8:6; 9:1 (2); 9:2; 9:5; 9:14; 10:21 (2); 10:22; 11:20; 11:23 (2); 11:26; 11:27 (2); 11:29; 11:32; 12:3; 12:5; 14:37; 15:31; 15:57; 15:58 (2); 16:7; 16:10; 16:19; 16:22 (2); 16:23

2 Corinthians: 1:2; 1:3; 1:14; 2:12; 3:16; 3:17 (2); 3:18 (2); 4:5; 4:14; 5:6; 5:8; 5:11; 8:5; 8:9; 8:19; 8:21; 10:8; 10:17; 10:18; 11:17; 11:31; 12:1; 12:8; 13:10; 13:14

Galatians: 1:3; 1:19; 5:10; 6:14; 6:18

Ephesians: 1:2; 1:3; 1:15; 1:17; 2:21; 3:11; 4:1; 4:5; 4:17; 5:8; 5:10; 5:17; 5:19; 5:20; 5:22; 6:1; 6:4; 6:7; 6:8; 6:10; 6:21; 6:23; 6:24

Philippians: 1:2; 1:14; 2:11; 2:19; 2:24; 2:29; 3:1; 3:8; 3:20; 4:1; 4:2; 4:4; 4:5; 4:10; 4:23

Colossians: 1:3; 1:10; 2:6; 3:13; 3:17; 3:18; 3:20; 3:22; 3:23; 3:24 (2); 4:7; 4:17

1 Thessalonians: 1:1; 1:3; 1:6; 1:8; 2:15; 2:19; 3:8; 3:11; 3:12; 3:13; 4:1; 4:2; 4:6; 4:15 (2); 4:16; 4:17 (2); 5:2; 5:9; 5:12; 5:23; 5:27; 5:28

2 Thessalonians: 1:1; 1:2; 1:7; 1:8; 1:9; 1:12 (2); 2:1; 2:2; 2:8; 2:13; 2:14; 2:16; 3:1; 3:3; 3:4; 3:5; 3:6; 3:12; 3:16 (2); 3:18

1 Timothy: 1:2; 1:12; 1:14; 6:3; 6:14; 6:15

2 Timothy: 1:2; 1:8; 1:16; 1:18 (2); 2:7; 2:19 (2); 2:22; 2:24; 3:11; 4:8; 4:14; 4:17; 4:18; 4:22

Philemon: 1:3; 1:5; 1:16; 1:20; 1:25

Hebrews: 2:3; 7:14; 13:20

James: 1:1; 2:1; 3:9; 4:10; 4:15; 5:7; 5:8; 5:14; 5:15

1 Peter: 1:3; 2:3; 2:13; 3:12 (2); 3:15

2 Peter: 1:2; 1:8; 1:11; 1:14; 1:16; 2:1; 2:9; 2:20; 3:2; 3:10; 3:18

Jude: 4; 5; 14; 17; 21; 25

Revelation: 1:8; 1:10; 11:8; 17:14; 19:16; 22:20; 22:21

Unclassifiable References to Members of the Trinity (25 total)

Matthew: 27:10

Luke: 1:9; 1:17 (2)

Acts: 5:9; 5:19; 8:26; 8:39; 12:23

1 Corinthians: 3:5; 3:20; 10:26; 11:11; 14:37

Hebrews: 1:10; 12:14; 13:6

James: 1:7; 5:10; 5:11 (2)

1 Peter: 1:25

Jude: 9

Revelation: 6:10; 14:13